U0920715

上海宋庆龄故居纪念馆 编

上海辞书出版社

策展小组

总策划：邵莉
项目统筹：麦灵芝
内容策划：王宁宁
学术指导：刘世襄
展品信息：麦灵芝、宫洁菁、王宁宁、符朋、陈钰彬
展品摄影：麦灵芝、宫洁菁、王宁宁、徐建华
文物保护：王宁宁、符朋

图录编委会

主编：宋时娟
副主编：宫洁菁
编辑：麦灵芝、王宁宁
撰文：王宁宁
美术编辑：陈婧、尤优

前言

宋庆龄这个光辉的名字，是和中国近百年的历史紧密相连的。她出生在19世纪末半殖民地半封建社会的旧中国，少年时远赴美国接受教育，青年时追随孙中山献身革命，为中国旧民主主义革命事业做出了独特贡献。孙中山逝世后，宋庆龄坚定地捍卫孙中山的革命理想和政策，从革命的民主主义者成长为一名共产主义战士，为人民解放、民族团结、国家统一建树了丰功伟绩，为国际友好、世界和平、人类进步与妇女儿童福利事业做出了卓越贡献。

2020年1月27日，为纪念中华人民共和国名誉主席宋庆龄同志诞辰127周年，上海宋庆龄故居纪念馆充分挖掘馆藏资源，策划推出“手泽如新 往事如诉——宋庆龄文物珍藏展”。展览选取了宋庆龄生平重要节点中具有代表性和故事性的200余件文物展品，涵盖宋庆龄在上海寓所遗留的历史照片、信函文稿、著作题词、国务礼品、生活用品等珍贵文物。展览六个版块分别由一张主题图片和一件主题文物统领，并以宋庆龄的原文原话引领文物组合。第一版块展示宋庆龄的求学历程和家庭背景，第二版块展示孙中山与宋庆龄相濡以沫的婚姻生活，第三版块展示宋庆龄捍卫民权、抵御侵略和投身解放事业的革命历程，第四版块展示宋庆龄为新中国建设、和平外交和妇儿福利事业做出的独特贡献，第五版块展示宋庆龄简约雅致的生活情趣，第六版块展示宋庆龄加入中国共产党的光辉历程。

今年，在展览的基础上，我们选取精美的文物图片，辅以翔实的文物说明，编著了《手泽如新 往事如诉——宋庆龄文物珍藏展图录》，力图通过对展出文物的微观研究，拼接还原历史的原貌，展现宋庆龄伟大光荣的一生。

抚今追昔，继往开来。让我们在全面建设社会主义现代化国家的新征程中，学习、继承和发扬宋庆龄的爱国思想、革命意志和情操风范，为实现中华民族伟大复兴的中国梦而努力奋斗。

上海宋庆龄故居纪念馆

二〇二二年七月

目录

P 40—67

（1913 年）当我从学院毕业回国时，正处于国内二次革命初期。我发现我父亲在日本政治避难，孙博士也在那里……他非常关心我的学习和活动，对我的工作鼓励甚多，使我不知不觉渐渐地被他所吸引，所以当他要求和我结婚时，我就同意了。

——1921 年宋庆龄自述

P 68—75

一旦我们所爱的人与我们诀别而去，那么相互爱得越深，我们所承受的悲痛也就更深沉……但正像你所说，我们终有甜蜜和爱恋的记忆留在心间。

——1975 年宋庆龄致廖梦醒信

P 76—89

现在，我认为我们背弃了孙中山领导群众和加强群众的政策，因此我只有暂时引退以待更贤明的政策出现。我对于革命并没有灰心。使我失望的，只是有些领导过革命的人已经走上了歧途。

——1927 年宋庆龄文稿《为抗议违反孙中山的革命原则和政策的声明》

P 90—105

我坚决相信，中国不但能够抵抗日本的任何侵略，并且能够而且必须准备收复失地。中国最大的力量在于中国人民大众已经觉醒起来了。

——1937 年宋庆龄文稿《中国是不可征服的》

P 106—117

（1945 年）保卫中国同盟的名称改为中国福利基金会。同时也宣布了这一组织的远景，它将扩大与发展，它将致力于遭受战争创伤的恢复与建设工作。

——1950 年宋庆龄文稿《中国福利基金会工作报告》

P 118—163

我可以告诉你，这里正在发生的一切令人振奋。孙中山先生的所有理想正在被有力地付诸实施。这些理想和其他一些重大的计划一起，使这里成为一个真正的崭新的中国。我们已确立了自己应有的地位，同世界上其他的伟大民族一同前进。

——1951 年宋庆龄致克劳特夫人信

P 164—181　宋庆龄曾说，去北京是上班，回上海则是回家，她把这里称为“可爱的家”。她在给友人的信中写道：“我刚刚到家，发现气候清爽，我很喜欢……我的小花园很怡人，有高大桉（樟）树，鸟儿在上面筑巢，清晨鸟儿们歌唱。我的管家说它们似乎知道我回家了，一直在歌唱！”

P 182—189　1981 年 5 月 15 日，中共中央政治局一致决定接收宋庆龄同志为中共正式党员。

宋庆龄(1893 — 1981)，中华人民共和国的缔造者之一，中华人民共和国名誉主席，爱国主义、民主主义、国际主义和共产主义的伟大战士，杰出的国际社会活动家，保卫世界和平事业久经考验的前驱，中国共产党的优秀党员。孙中山夫人。

上海宋庆龄故居是宋庆龄居住时间最长的地方，也是她进行国务活动的重要场所。这里留下的文物，真实地记录了宋庆龄浓厚深沉的亲情，记录了她精诚无间的爱情，记录了她简约雅致的生活。这里留下的文物，静静地讲述着宋庆龄为中国革命事业建树的不朽功绩，讲述着她为保卫世界和平、促进社会进步和人类幸福进行的不懈奋斗，讲述着她为中华人民共和国的建立、建设做出的独特贡献。

宋庆龄的家国情怀、高尚品格和革命精神，永远激励着我们在实现中华民族伟大复兴中国梦的征途上砥砺前行。

Soong Ching Ling(1893-1981), wife of Dr. Sun Yat-sen, was one of the founders of the People's Republic of China, the Honorary Chairman of the People's Republic of China, and a great fighter of patriotism, democracy, internationalism and communism,an outstanding international social activist, a proven pioneer in the cause of defending world peace, an outstanding member of the Communist Party of China.

Soong Ching Ling's former residence in Shanghai is the place where she had lived for the longest time in her life, and was also an important place for her to conduct affairs of state. The relics reflect Soong Ching Ling's affection for her family, her love, and her lifestyle. These exhibits speak to us of Soong Ching Ling's contributions to China's revolutionary cause, her efforts to the world peace, social progress, and human happiness, and her unique contribution in the founding and reconstruction of the People's Republic of China.

Soong Ching Ling's patriotism, noble character and revolutionary spirit will always inspire us to forge ahead on the journey of realizing the Chinese dream of the great rejuvenation of the Chinese nation.

宋庆龄文物珍藏展

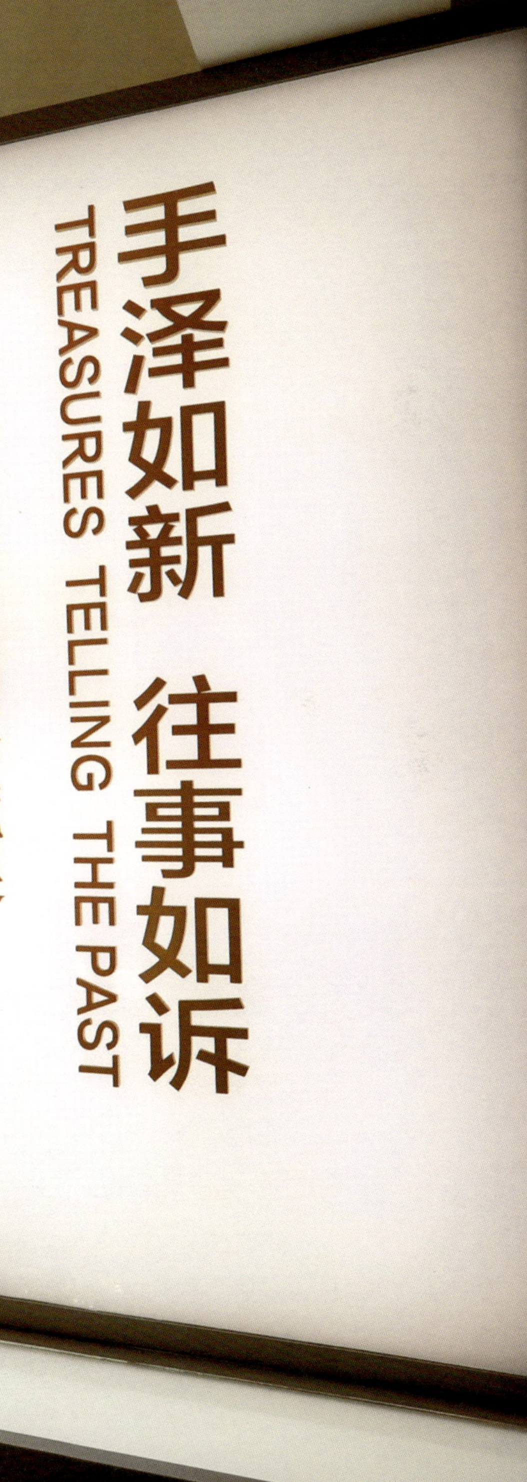
手泽如新 往事如诉
TREASURES TELLING THE PAST
宋庆龄文物珍藏展
EXHIBITION OF SOONG CHING LING'S RELICS

1908 年

1920 年

1927 年

20 世纪 20 年代

1929 年

1929 年

1937 年

1938 年

1944 年

1956 年

1957 年

1958 年

我在家读书，一直到12岁才被送入教会学校，我的父母都是基督教徒。我在中西女塾就读，直到我有了出洋留学的机会。在（美国）新泽西州和南部当了两年家庭教师之后，我进了佐治亚州梅肯的威斯里安女子学院。

——1921年宋庆龄自述

Since my parents are Christians, I was sent to a mission school when I was 12 years old. Before that I was studying at home. I had been studying at Mc Tyeire School until I got the opportunity to study abroad. After working as a home teacher for two years in New Jersey and south of the United States, I was enrolled by Wesleyan College in Macon, Georgia.

——Self-introduction by Soong Ching Ling in 1921

1907 年宋庆龄在上海的留影

A photo of Soong Ching Ling in Shanghai in 1907

● 1893 年 1 月 27 日宋庆龄出生在上海。此照为 1907 年宋庆龄出国留学前在上海留影，由上海岩本照相馆拍摄，被宋庆龄用作 1907 年赴美护照证件照片。

宋庆龄儿时佩戴的香袋 （李云 捐赠）

The perfume satchel worn by Soong Ching Ling in her childhood

宋庆龄保存的中西女塾旧照

A photo of Mc Tyeire School preserved by Soong Ching Ling

●宋庆龄1902年至1907年在中西女塾就读。中西女塾创办于1892年，是以教授西学为主的教会学校。1917年，中西女塾从汉口路西藏路口迁至江苏路，此照片中的建筑为当时的教学楼。为纪念去世的第二任校长莲吉生，该教学楼后被命名为“莲吉生堂”。中西女塾于1930年更名为中西女中，中华人民共和国成立后与圣玛利亚女中合并，成为上海市第三女子中学。

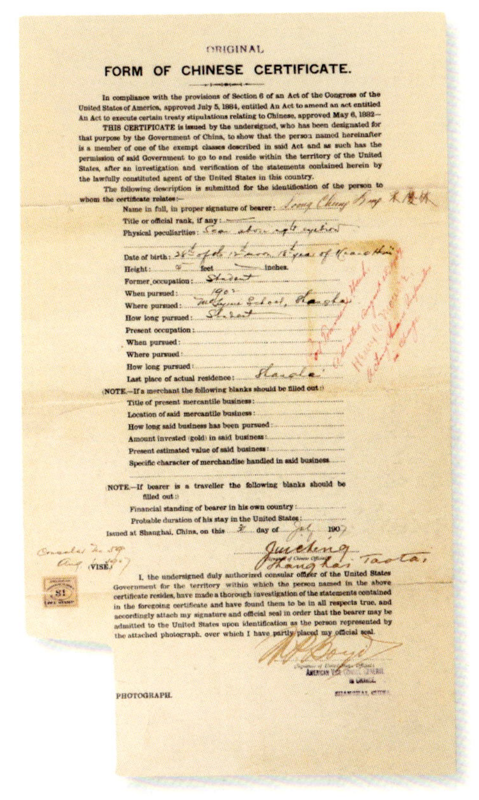

ORIGINAL

FORM OF CHINESE CERTIFICATE.

In compliance with the provisions of Section 6 of an Act of the Congress of the United States of America, approved July 5, 1884, entitled An Act to amend an act entitled An Act to execute certain treaty stipulations relating to Chinese, approved May 6, 1882—

THIS CERTIFICATE is issued by the undersigned, who has been designated for that purpose by the Government of China, to show that the person named hereinafter is a member of one of the exempt classes described in said Act and as such has the permission of said Government to go to and reside within the territory of the United States, after an investigation and verification of the statements contained herein by the lawfully constituted agent of the United States in this country.

The following description is submitted for the identification of the person to whom the certificate relates:—

Name in full, in proper signature of bearer:

Title or official rank, if any:

Physical peculiarities:

Date of birth:

Height: feet inches.

Former occupation:

When pursued:

Where pursued:

How long pursued:

Present occupation:

When pursued:

Where pursued:

How long pursued:

Last place of actual residence:

(NOTE.—If a merchant the following blanks should be filled out:)

Title of present mercantile business:

Location of said mercantile business:

How long said business has been pursued:

Amount invested (gold) in said business:

Present estimated value of said business:

Specific character of merchandise handled in said business

(NOTE.—If bearer is a traveller the following blanks should be filled out:)

Financial standing of bearer in his own country:

Probable duration of his stay in the United States:

Issued at Shanghai, China, on this day of 190

(VISE.)

I, the undersigned duly authorized consular officer of the United States Government for the territory within which the person named in the above certificate resides, have made a thorough investigation of the statements contained in the foregoing certificate and have found them to be in all respects true, and accordingly attach my signature and official seal in order that the bearer may be admitted to the United States upon identification as the person represented by the attached photograph, over which I have partly placed my official seal.

PHOTOGRAPH.

1907 年宋庆龄赴美国留学护照　　　（周谷　捐赠）

Soong Ching Ling's passport for her study in the United States in 1907

● 1907 年，宋庆龄通过了清政府的官方出国留学考核，成为中国首批公费留美的女学生之一。此件为宋庆龄赴美留学护照正本，由正反两面构成。正面为中文，记录了护照编号为“新字第叁佰贰拾肆号”，由清政府江南海关道 1907 年 7 月（清光绪三十三年六月）签发；反面为英文，记录了宋庆龄的中英文姓名、出生日期、身高、体貌特征等信息，可知宋庆龄 1907 年 8 月 1 日获得美国驻沪总领事馆入境许可签证，8 月 28 日由美国华盛顿州汤森堡入境。护照上所列中文姓名“宋庆林”系宋庆龄早期用名，下方证件照被剪。宋庆龄赴美留学护照副本现存于美国国家档案馆西雅图分馆。

宋庆龄在美国留学时与友人的合影

Photos of Soong Ching Ling with her friends in the United States

●宋庆龄 1908 年考入美国佐治亚州梅肯市的威斯里安女子学院（Wesleyan College），主修文学专业。这两张照片为宋庆龄 1913 年离美赴日前夕与友人合影。

1913 年宋庆龄与宋子文、宋美龄、牛惠生、牛惠珠合影

A photo of Soong Ching Ling, Tse-vung Soong, Soong May Ling, Way-sung New, and Way-tsu New in the United States in 1913

● 1913 年宋庆龄（左二）在离美赴日前夕，与大弟宋子文（左一）、妹妹宋美龄（左五），表兄牛惠生（左四）、表妹牛惠珠（左三）在波士顿留影。牛惠生、牛惠珠为倪珪金（宋庆龄母亲倪珪贞的姐姐）和牛尚周夫妇的孩子。

宋庆龄、宋蔼龄、宋美龄三姐妹在美国留学时留影
Photos of the Soong sisters when studying in the United States

● 1907 年，宋庆龄偕妹妹宋美龄赴美留学。在新泽西州萨密特镇的波特温学校注册学习一年后，两人于 1908 年 9 月入学佐治亚州梅肯市的威斯里安女子学院，与 1904 年来此求学的大姐宋蔼龄同校。1909 年，宋蔼龄毕业回国，宋美龄转入佐治亚州德马雷斯特镇的皮德蒙特学校就读，后于 1910 年重返威斯里安女子学院，继续与宋庆龄同校。1913 年，宋庆龄毕业离美，宋美龄进入马萨诸塞州威尔斯利学院（Wellesley College），于 1917 年毕业回国。

THE GREATEST EVENT OF THE TWENTIETH CENTURY

ONE of the greatest events of the twentieth century, the greatest event since Waterloo, in the opinion of many well-known educators and politicians, is the Chinese Revolution. It is a most glorious achievement. It means the emancipation of four hundred million souls from the thraldom of an absolute monarchy, which has been in existence for over four thousand years, and under whose rule "life, liberty, and the pursuit of happiness," have been denied. It also signifies the downfall of a dynasty whose cruel extortions and selfishness have reduced the once prosperous nation to a poverty-stricken country. The overthrowing of the Manchu government means the destruction and expulsion of a court where the most barbaric customs, and degrading morals were in existence.

Five months ago our wildest dream could not have been for a republic. To some, even the promise of an early constitutional government was received with skepticism. But deep down in the heart of every patriotic Chinese, were he a politician or a laborer, there was the anti-Manchu spirit. All the sufferings, such as famine, flood, and retrogression in every phase of life was traced to the tyrannical Manchus, and their court of dishonest officials. Oppression was the cause of this wonderful revolution which came as a blessing in disguise.

Already we are witnessing reforms that would never have been accomplished under a despot. We read in the papers of the queueless movement in China, and how thousands and thousands have sacrificed their appendages—the Chinese national disgrace. To appreciate this fact, which seems so commonplace to the matter-of-fact foreigner, we must remember that the queue is a trait or a characteristic of centuries, and that the Chinese are the most conservative people in the world. They love to adhere

to old customs, and up to six months ago the queue, which was their most striking mark of distinction from the rest of the civilized world, was carefully cherished. Ten years ago, the number of queueless heads could be counted on the fingers. No one who expected to hold governmental offices dared to cut off his queue. Such an act was regarded as being anti-Manchu, therefore it was revolutionary. But now the anti-Manchu spirit is the order of the day in China, and the number of heads with queues can be counted on the fingers. There are innumerable other reforms that are now taking place in China; among them are the social, educational, and industrial reorganizations. Since order is restored, the Currency Problem and the Taxation Question will be the next problems to be solved. We are firm in our belief, with the knowledge of the glorious success of other important reforms that the Chinese are capable and efficient to deal with these intelligently, to the prosperity and integrity of that ancient empire.

The Revolution has established in China Liberty and Equality, those two inalienable rights of the individual which have caused the loss of so many noble and heroic lives, but there is still Fraternity to be acquired. Dean Crawshaw of Colgate University said in one of his lectures, that Fraternity is the yet unrealized ideal of humanity, and that Liberty has no safe foundation except human brotherhood, and that real Equality can never be anything but a dream until men feel towards each other as brothers. In fact, he said Fraternity is the basis of both Liberty and Equality, therefore it should be the purpose of the 20th century to foster that ideal.

And it may be for China, the oldest of nations, to point the way to this Fraternity. In other ways, too, China will take her place in the effort to uplift humanity. Napoleon Bonaparte said, "When China moves, she will move the world. "The realization of that statement does not seem to be far off. A race amounting to one-quarter of the world's population, and inhabiting the largest empire on the globe, whose civilization displays so many manifestations of excellence cannot help but be influential in the uplifting of

mankind. China was the first possessor of a criminal code; her philosophers gave to the world some of the noblest contributions to human thinking; while her extensive literature which has delighted and won the admiration of those learned Europeans who spent their lifetime in the exclusive study of China and her exquisite code of Social and Moral Ethics are hardly paralleled elsewhere. For centuries the Chinese have been a peace-loving people. To them the pen is mightier than the sword. They have esteemed the arts of peace, and neglected the arts of war, worshipped the scholar and slighted the soldier. Sir Robert Hart said: "They believe in right so firmly that they scorn to think it requires to be supported or enforced by might. These qualities are not to be found simply in isolated cases, but are characteristic of the race as a whole." Mr. Conger, the United States ex-minister to China, has said that "If civilization means, as it should, the highest sensibility of the conscience of man, there is in China the highest civilization to be found in the world." China, with its multitudinous population, and its love of peace—love in the real essence of the word—shall stand forth as the incarnation of Peace. It cannot but be instrumental in bringing about that humanitarian movement—Universal Peace—when Rights need not be backed by armies and "dreadnaughts," and all political disagreements will be, at last, settled by the Hague Tribunal.

—Chung-ling Soong, '13.

1912 年 4 月《威斯里安》院刊上发表的宋庆龄文章《二十世纪最伟大的事件》

The Greatest Event of the Twentieth Century by Soong Ching Ling published in *the Wesleyan* in April 1912

●身处异国他乡，宋庆龄关心祖国命运，关注国内政治。获知辛亥革命胜利的消息后，她充满激情地写下《二十世纪最伟大的事件》一文，为“四万万人民从君主专制制度的奴役下解放了出来”而欢欣鼓舞。该文发表在《威斯里安》院刊 1912 年 4 月号上。

宋庆龄保存的大学母校威斯里安女子学院影集

A photo album of Wesleyan College preserved by Soong Ching Ling

●宋庆龄一直保存着母校威斯里安女子学院的影集。影集内有照片 15 张，这两张照片展示了威斯里安女子学院建筑的外景。

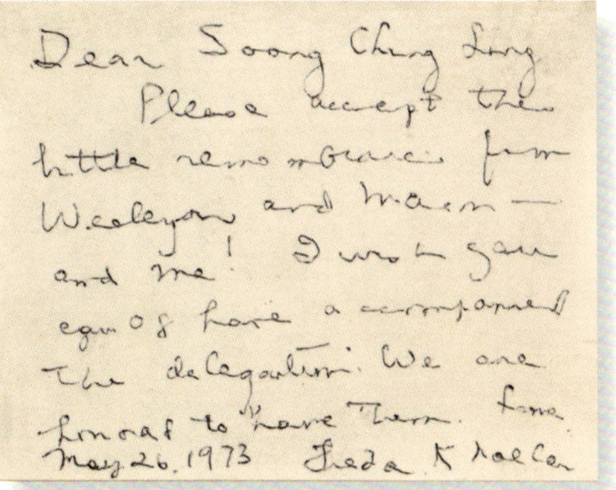

Dear Soong Ching Ling
Please accept this
little remembrance from
Wesleyan and Macon —
and me! I wish you
could have accompanied
the delegation. We are
fortunate to have them. [illegible]
May 26, 1973 Freda K [illegible]

宋庆龄保存的威斯里安女子学院校徽

A badge of Wesleyan College preserved by Soong Ching Ling

● 1973 年 5 月 26 日，宋庆龄的大学校友赠送给她一枚威斯里安女子学院校徽。校徽上部分拉丁文意为：“学问与虔诚，佐治亚，梅肯，威斯里安学院（SCIENTIA ET PIETAS, WESLEYAN COLLEGE MACON GEORGIA）”。所附字条谓“请接受这枚纪念品”。字条信封图案为威斯里安女子学院 1836 年注册成立时的校舍。

Senatus Wesleyani Collegii

Omnibus has litteras perlecturis salutem.

Notum sit Rosamonde Chung-ling Soong in Litterarum et Scientiarum studia, necnon in cetera hujus Collegii officia diligenter feliciterque incubuisse. Quamobrem Praeses et Professores, consentientibus Honorandis Reverendisque Curatoribus, pro auctoritate sibi commissa, eam titulo gradique Artium Baccalaureae condecoraverunt, eique omnia jura, honores et insignia ubique gentium ad eundem gradum pertinentia contulerunt.

Cujus Rei hae litterae, sub Collegii sigillo subscriptisque praesidis et professorum chirographis datae testimonio sint.

Ex Aedibus Collegii Macone in Georgia, die sexto et vicesimo Maii MCMXIII

宋庆龄的大学毕业证书

Diploma issued by Wesleyan College to Soong Ching Ling

● 1913 年 5 月，宋庆龄以优异的成绩从威斯里安女子学院毕业，获文学学士学位。此为学院 1913 年 5 月 26 日签发给她的毕业证书。证书为拉丁文，下方有学院教师署名。

宋庆龄一生充满着对家的眷恋，她保存着许多家人的物品，是她对亲情的思念，更是对祖国统一的企盼。1979 年国庆前夕她深情地写道：“在举国欢庆祖国伟大节日的时刻，我不能不想念台湾的骨肉同胞。三十年了，台湾归回祖国、实现国家统一的大业还没有完成，哪一个中国人不应感到身有责任呢？”

Soong Ching Ling maintained kinship with her family throughout her life. She preserved many kinsfolk belongings to remember domestic affection and pray for the reunification of China. On the eve of National Day in 1979, she wrote affectionately: “I can't help but miss the compatriots in Taiwan on this day when the whole country is celebrating the great festival of the motherland. Thirty years have passed already since Taiwan's separation. National reunification has not yet been completed. Should not each Chinese feel responsible?”

宋庆龄幼年时与家人合影

A Photo of Soong Ching Ling with her parents and siblings

●此照为目前可见最早的宋庆龄全家合影，由上海耀华照相馆（SZE YUEN MING & CO. Shanghai）拍摄。照片左侧为宋庆龄父亲宋耀如，右侧为母亲倪珪贞。左侧端坐及中间站立的幼童推测为倪珪贞的长子（早殇）和长女宋蔼龄，倪珪贞怀抱的婴童为宋庆龄，是目前可见宋庆龄最早的影像记录。耀华照相馆是上海早期照相业“四大天王”之一，由清末著名商业摄影师施德之创建。

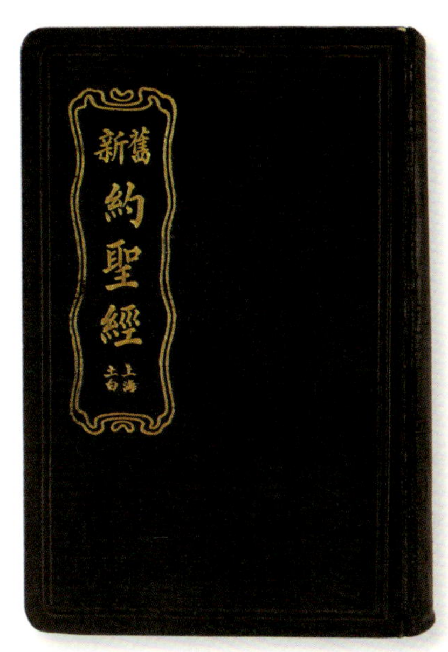

宋庆龄家人使用过的十字架项链和沪语版《旧新约圣经》

Necklace with a cross and *the Old and New Testaments of the Bible* of Shanghai colloquial version used by Soong Ching Ling's family

---

●宋庆龄父母均为基督教徒，宋庆龄保存了部分家人遗留的宗教用品。十字架项链上镂刻浮雕梅花图案，由杨庆和银楼生产。沪语版《旧新约圣经》由上海美华圣经会1928年出版。

宋庆龄的父亲宋耀如

Soong Ching Ling's father Charles Jones Soong

●宋耀如（1861 — 1918），字嘉树。早年在美国谋生，后回国传教，创办实业，是孙中山的追随者、挚友和他革命事业的赞助者。1915 年 4 月宋耀如在东京摄影留念，将此照寄赠在美国留学的宋子文。宋耀如在照片背面用英文写着："To Tsvung with love from father, Tokio, April 4th, 1915."（给子文，爱你的父亲。1915 年 4 月 4 日于东京。）

宋庆龄的母亲倪珪贞

Soong Ching Ling's mother Ni Kwei-tseng

●倪珪贞（1869 — 1931），出生于江苏省川沙县(今属上海市浦东新区)基督教传教士家庭，自幼信教，幼时入家塾读书，15 岁入读上海西门裨文女学，毕业后留校担任教员。1887 年倪珪贞与宋耀如结婚，婚后主持家政，教育子女，支持丈夫资助革命事业。

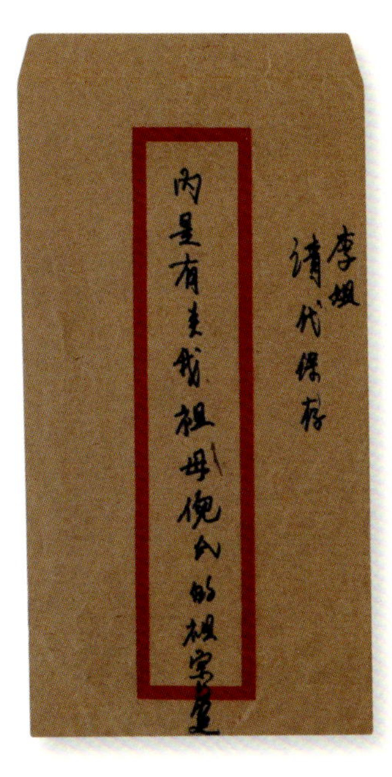

李姆
请代保存

内是有关我祖母倪氏的祖宗史

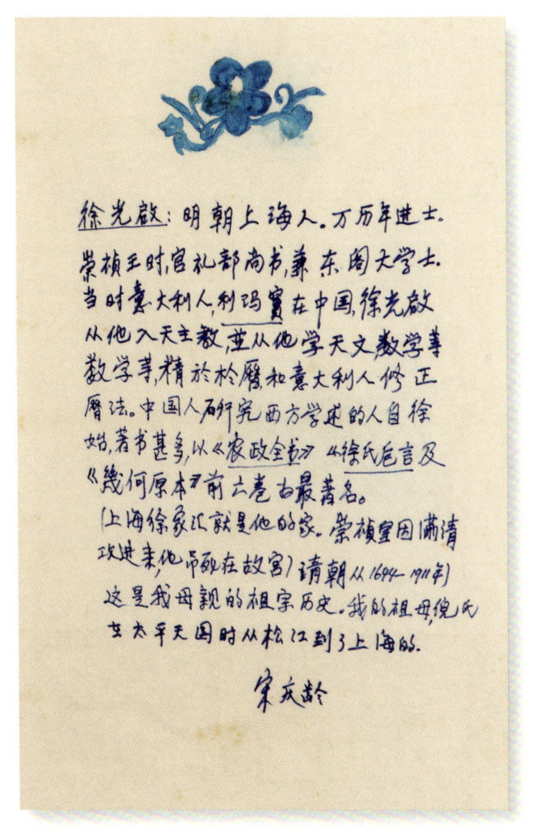

徐光啟：明朝上海人。万历年进士。
崇祯王时，官礼部尚书，兼东阁大学士。
当时意大利人，利玛竇在中国，徐光啟
从他入天主教，并从他学天文数学等
数学等，精於於曆和意大利人修正
曆法。中国人研究西方学述的人自徐
始，著书甚多，以《农政全书》《徐氏庖言及
《幾何原本》前六卷为最著名。
（上海徐家汇就是他的家。崇祯皇因满清
攻进来，他吊死在故宫）清朝从1644—1911年）
这是我母親的祖宗历史。我的祖母倪氏
在太平天国时从松江到了上海的。

宋庆龄

宋庆龄手书的外祖母家史

The family history of maternal grandmother, written by Soong Ching Ling

---

●此信为宋庆龄手书的母亲一族系徐光启后代的家史，交由保姆李燕娥收藏。

1917 年宋庆龄全家在上海合影

A photo of the Soong family in Shanghai in 1917

● 1917 年 7 月，宋子文和宋美龄从美国回到上海，在上海霞飞路（原宝昌路、今淮海中路）491 号家中合影留念。该照是目前所见唯一一张宋氏全家照。

宋耀如、倪珪贞的六个子女依次为：宋蔼龄（二排左）、宋庆龄（二排右）、宋子文（二排中）、宋美龄（后排右）、宋子良（后排左）、宋子安（前排）。

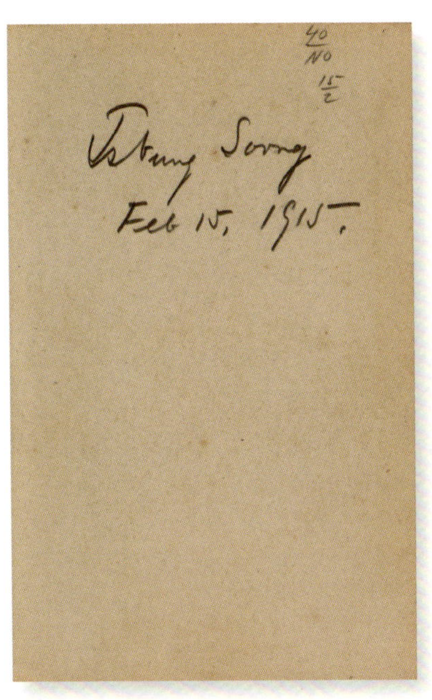

宋子文留学美国期间读过的《德国经济》
Germany Economy used by Tse-vung Soong during he studied in the U.S.A

●宋子文(1894—1971),宋庆龄大弟,历任广州国民政府、武汉国民政府和南京国民政府要职。此书是他留学美国期间读过的德文版的《德国经济》。宋子文于1912年赴美,先进入范德比尔特大学,但在未完成注册之前即转赴波士顿入读哈佛大学,主修经济学。1915年宋子文从哈佛大学毕业后,前往纽约入读哥伦比亚大学进修研究生课程,于1917年完成学业,离美回国。《德国经济》一书节选埃德加·洛宁的《德意志帝国宪法的基本原则》和保罗·昂特的《德国在世界经济中的地位》的部分章节,由美国布鲁克林东区高中现代语言部主席约翰·博尔编辑注释,1910年由纽约亨利·霍尔特公司出版。内页有宋子文签名"Ts Vung Soong Feb 15,1915."(宋子文1915年2月15日)。

两广盐务稽核所全体职员赠宋子文银盾

A silver shield presented to Tse-vung Soong by the staff of Guangdong-Guangxi Salt Inspectorate

---

●宋子文曾于1923年担任两广盐务稽核所经理，1924年任中央银行行长，其后调任广东省政府商务厅厅长。此为两广盐务稽核所全体职员贺宋子文任广东省政府商务厅厅长所赠银盾，银盾上写有“利用厚生”字样，意为物尽其用，富裕民生。

1913年，根据袁世凯善后借款合同设立的盐务稽核所成立。以孙中山为首的革命党人从一开始就反对北洋政府的善后借款和盐务稽核所。1923年广东革命政府派人接管广东稽核分所，不久将其改称两广盐务稽核所。1926年4月，广州国民政府裁撤两广盐务稽核所，将其与两广盐运使公署并为盐务总处。

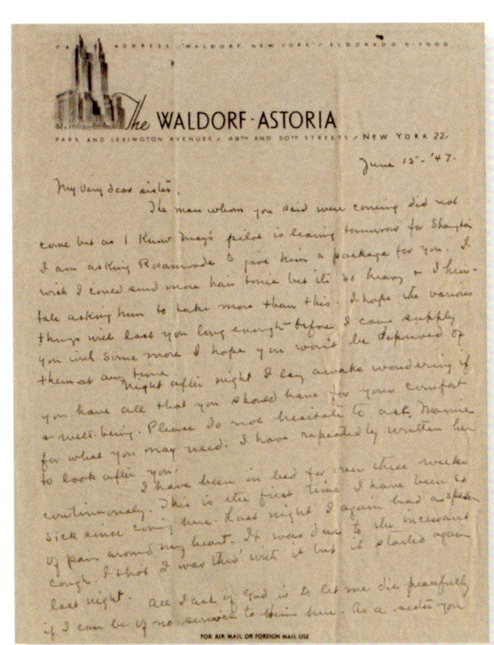

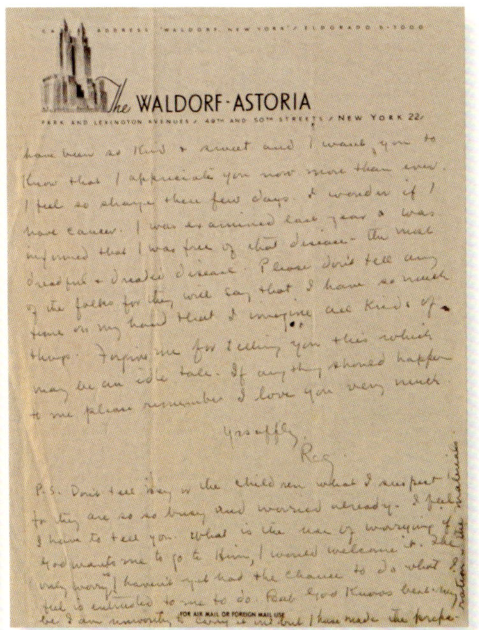

1947 年 6 月 15 日宋蔼龄致宋庆龄信

A letter from Soong Ai Ling to Soong Ching Ling on June 15, 1947

●宋蔼龄（1889 — 1973），宋庆龄姐姐，孔祥熙夫人。此件为 1947 年 6 月 15 日宋蔼龄自美国纽约致宋庆龄信，信中写道：“作为妹妹，你一直是那么和蔼和可爱，我想要你知道现在我比以前更加喜欢你了。”信末署名 Reg 是宋蔼龄的英文昵称。

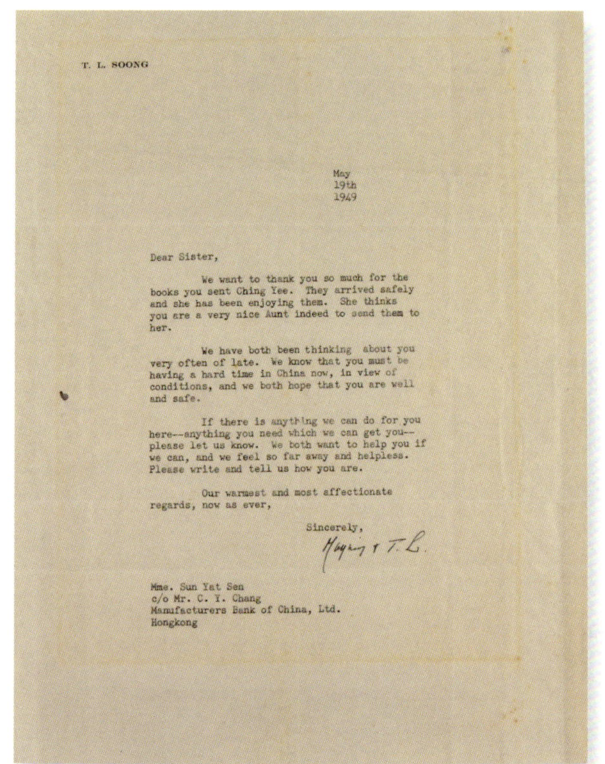

T. L. SOONG

May
19th
1949

Dear Sister,

We want to thank you so much for the books you sent Ching Yee. They arrived safely and she has been enjoying them. She thinks you are a very nice Aunt indeed to send them to her.

We have both been thinking about you very often of late. We know that you must be having a hard time in China now, in view of conditions, and we both hope that you are well and safe.

If there is anything we can do for you here--anything you need which we can get you--please let us know. We both want to help you if we can, and we feel so far away and helpless. Please write and tell us how you are.

Our warmest and most affectionate regards, now as ever,

Sincerely,

Mayling & T. L.

Mme. Sun Yat Sen
c/o Mr. C. Y. Chang
Manufacturers Bank of China, Ltd.
Hongkong

1949 年 5 月 19 日宋美龄、宋子良致宋庆龄信

A letter from Soong May Ling and Tse-liang Soong to Soong Ching Ling on May 19, 1949

●宋美龄（1898 — 2003），宋庆龄妹妹，蒋介石夫人。宋子良（1899 — 1987），宋庆龄二弟。此件为 1949 年 5 月 19 日宋美龄、宋子良致宋庆龄信，由中国（香港）制造商银行的 C.Y.Chang 先生转交宋庆龄。来信表达了对宋庆龄的挂念，写道："最近，我们都经常想起你，考虑到目前的局势，我们知道你在中国的生活一定很艰苦，希望你能平安、顺利。"信末有两人英文署名"May Ling & T. L."

蒋介石题字纹瓷碟

A dish with Chiang Kai-shek's inscription pattern

●蒋介石（1887 — 1975），宋庆龄妹夫，历任黄埔军校校长、国民革命军总司令、国民政府主席等职。1926 年 10 月 10 日，国民革命军北伐攻克武昌，后广州国民政府迁都武汉。为纪念这次重大胜利，追思牺牲的革命烈士，时任国民革命军总司令的蒋介石亲笔题词“克复武汉 先烈之血 主义之花”，并下令以其名义依其所书蓝本于景德镇烧制一套瓷器赠予国民革命军留念，器型包括碗碟、花盆等，此为其中一件，是见证北伐战争的珍贵实物。

1927 年蒋介石与宋美龄结婚时友人赠送的台钟

A table clock presented to Chiang Kai-shek and Soong May Ling as their wedding gift in 1927

● 1927 年 12 月蒋介石、宋美龄在上海结婚，此瑞士“尊皇”牌台钟为香港台商会领袖李星衢、黄砥江赠送的贺礼。台钟背面刻有“介石先生 美龄女士结婚志喜　香港李星衢 黄砥江敬贺”字样。

宋子良的照相机

A camera used by Tse-liang Soong

●宋子良，历任南京国民政府外交部秘书及总务司司长、广东省政府委员兼财政厅厅长、中国银行董事等职。此件宋子良的照相机由德国相机制造商科特·本津（Curt Bentzin）制造。

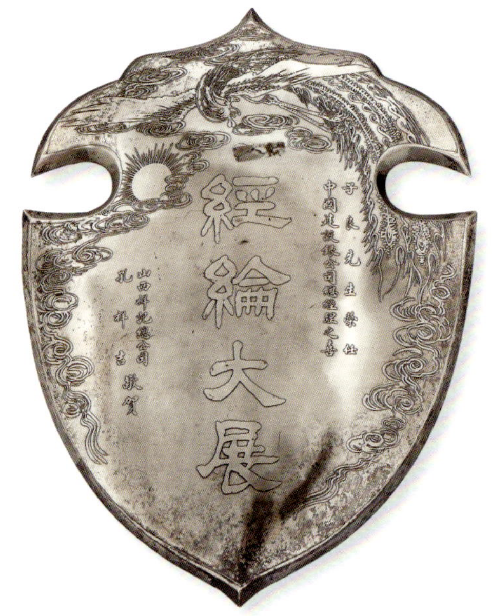

孔祥吉赠宋子良“经纶大展”银盾

A silver shield presented to Tse-liang Soong by Kung Hsiang-chi

●此件为孔祥熙（宋庆龄姐夫）堂弟、山西祥记总公司总经理孔祥吉祝贺宋子良任中国建设银公司总经理赠送的银盾，写有“经纶大展”字样，意为施展才能。

1932年宋庆龄与宋子良、宋子安在上海留影
A Photo of Soong Ching Ling with Tse-liang Soong and Tse-an Soong in Shanghai in 1932

● 1932年春，宋庆龄与弟弟宋子良（左一）、宋子安（右一）在上海出游时留影。

1932年宋庆龄与宋子安在父母墓前合影
A Photo of Soong Ching Ling with Tse-an Soong in front of the tomb of their parents in 1932

● 1931年8月，宋母倪珪贞葬于万国公墓宋耀如墓旁。次年8月，宋氏子女为父母共立合葬墓。建墓立碑之前，宋庆龄偕三弟宋子安同往万国公墓拜谒父母墓地，并合影留念。

宋子安赠送友人的银香炉

A silver incense burner presented by Tse-an Soong to his friend

●宋子安（1906 — 1969），历任中国建设银公司总经理、中国国货银行监察、香港广东银行董事会主席等职。此件为宋子安祝贺友人母亲六十寿辰赠送的银香炉，腹身写有“胡母张太夫人六旬荣庆 南极星辉 宋子安谨贺” 字样。

宋美龄贺母亲六十寿辰所写的“福寿全”条幅

A scroll with her mother's 60th birthday greetings *Fu Shou Quan* written by Soong May Ling

● 1928 年 6 月，倪珪贞六十寿辰，宋美龄为母亲手书“福寿全”条幅。这是目前仅见的宋美龄早期书法作品。

友人为倪珪贞贺寿所写的条幅

A scroll with Ni Kwei-tseng's birthday greetings written by a friend

●倪珪贞六十寿辰时，友人江长川为贺寿撰写“冠洪范九五福称觥舞彩林壬共祝寿无量”条幅。

江长川，上海人，中华全国基督教协进会副会长。

（1913 年）当我从学院毕业回国时，正处于国内二次革命初期。我发现我父亲在日本政治避难，孙博士也在那里……他非常关心我的学习和活动，对我的工作鼓励甚多，使我不知不觉渐渐地被他所吸引，所以当他要求和我结婚时，我就同意了。

——1921 年宋庆龄自述

When I graduated from college and returned to China（in 1913）, China was in the early stage of the Second Revolution. My father was taking refuge in Japan, and so was Dr. Sun… Dr. Sun cared so much about my studies and activities, and encouraged me so much in my work that I was gradually attracted to him. Therefore, when he proposed to marry me, I agreed.

——Self-introduction by Soong Ching Ling in 1921

孙中山与宋庆龄结婚纪念照

Dr. Sun Yat-sen and Soong Ching Ling after marriage

● 1915 年 10 月 25 日，孙中山、宋庆龄在日本东京结婚。1916 年 4 月 24 日，孙中山、宋庆龄由梅屋庄吉夫人陪同，前往东京大武照相馆拍摄了此照。

孔祥熙赠宋庆龄的结婚纪念银碗

A silver bowl presented to Soong Ching Ling by Kung Hsiang-hsi as a wedding gift

●此件为 1915 年 10 月 25 日宋庆龄的姐夫孔祥熙赠送她的结婚礼物。英文款识镌刻 “TO Mrs. Sun Wen, PRESENTED BY CHAUNCEY H. KUNG, 25TH, OCT,1915”（致孙文夫人，孔祥熙赠，1915 年 10 月 25 日）。

孙中山、宋庆龄与亲友在上海莫利爱路寓所合影

Dr. Sun Yat-sen and Soong Ching Ling with relatives and friends in their residence on Rue Molière, Shanghai

● 20世纪20年代初，宋庆龄（后排左二）、孙中山（后排左一）与母亲倪珪贞（后排左三）等在上海莫利爱路29号（今香山路7号）寓所餐厅留影。前排左起为廖承志、宋子文，二排中坐者为廖梦醒，后排右起依次为孔祥熙、宋蔼龄、宋美龄。

1922 年 1 月 2 日，孙中山、宋庆龄与中国国民党广西支部同志合影

Dr. Sun Yat-sen and Soong Ching Ling with comrades of KMT Guangxi branch on January 2, 1922

● 1921 年 12 月 4 日，孙中山在广西桂林设立北伐大本营，准备次年春入湘，大举北伐。宋庆龄亦于 12 月从广州抵桂林，协助孙中山开展工作。1922 年 1 月 2 日，宋庆龄陪同孙中山在桂林视察中国国民党广西支部。前排中坐者为孙中山、宋庆龄，右起为随同孙中山北伐的桂林督办邓家彦和夫人谢兰馨。

帝政取消一笑會

民國十一年六月
九日攝於
桂林疊綵山

This is the first airplane built in China. Designed May 1923.
Flown July 1923.
The "Rosamonde" (named in honor of
Mrs Sun Yat-sen)

宋庆龄与孙中山结婚后，成为孙中山的伴侣和助手，他们相濡以沫，共同走过十年的风雨征程

After marriage, Soong Ching Ling became a lifelong partner and assistant to Dr. Sun Yat-sen. They supported each other in a decade sharing weal and woe

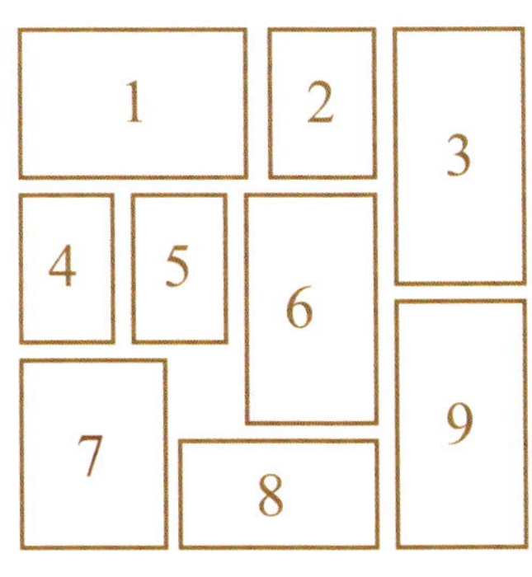

1. 1916 年 4 月 9 日孙中山、宋庆龄、廖仲恺、何香凝等和日本友人在东京举行帝政取消一笑会留影
2. 1918 年 3 月孙中山与宋庆龄在广州大元帅府
3. 1924 年 6 月 16 日孙中山与宋庆龄在黄埔军校
4. 1922 年 2 月孙中山与宋庆龄在广西桂林叠彩山
5. 1924 年 11 月 24 日孙中山与宋庆龄抵达日本神户
6. 1919 年冬孙中山与宋庆龄在上海结婚四周年合影
7. 1920 年 10 月孙中山与宋庆龄结婚五周年纪念照
8. 1923 年 8 月孙中山与宋庆龄在中国自行设计的飞机“洛士文”号前
9. 1924 年 1 月 1 日孙中山与宋庆龄出席在广州大元帅府举行的元旦庆祝会

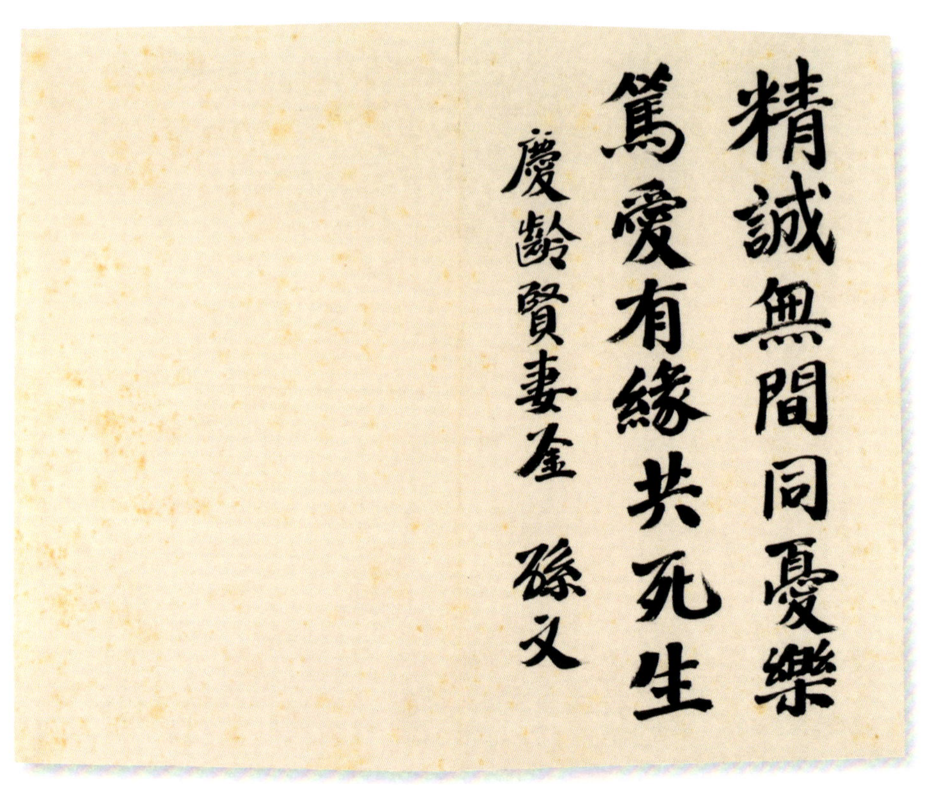

孙中山题赠宋庆龄的“精诚无间同忧乐 笃爱有缘共死生”册页

A couplet in Dr. Sun Yat-sen's handwritting: *To Ching Ling, my beloved wife. Sharing weal and woe in utmost sincerity / Sharing life and death in true love*

● 1922 年 6 月 16 日，被孙中山视作革命同志的陈炯明在广州发动武装叛乱，围攻观音山总统府。生死关头，宋庆龄临危不惧，再三婉求孙中山先走，坚持留下吸引叛军的火力让孙中山安全脱险。她同战士在敌人的炮火中沉着应战，经过一天一夜的艰难路程冲出层层封锁。在脱险过程中，宋庆龄不幸流产。此后，孙中山挥毫题赠宋庆龄此联，表达了他们夫妇同生死、共患难的恩爱情怀。

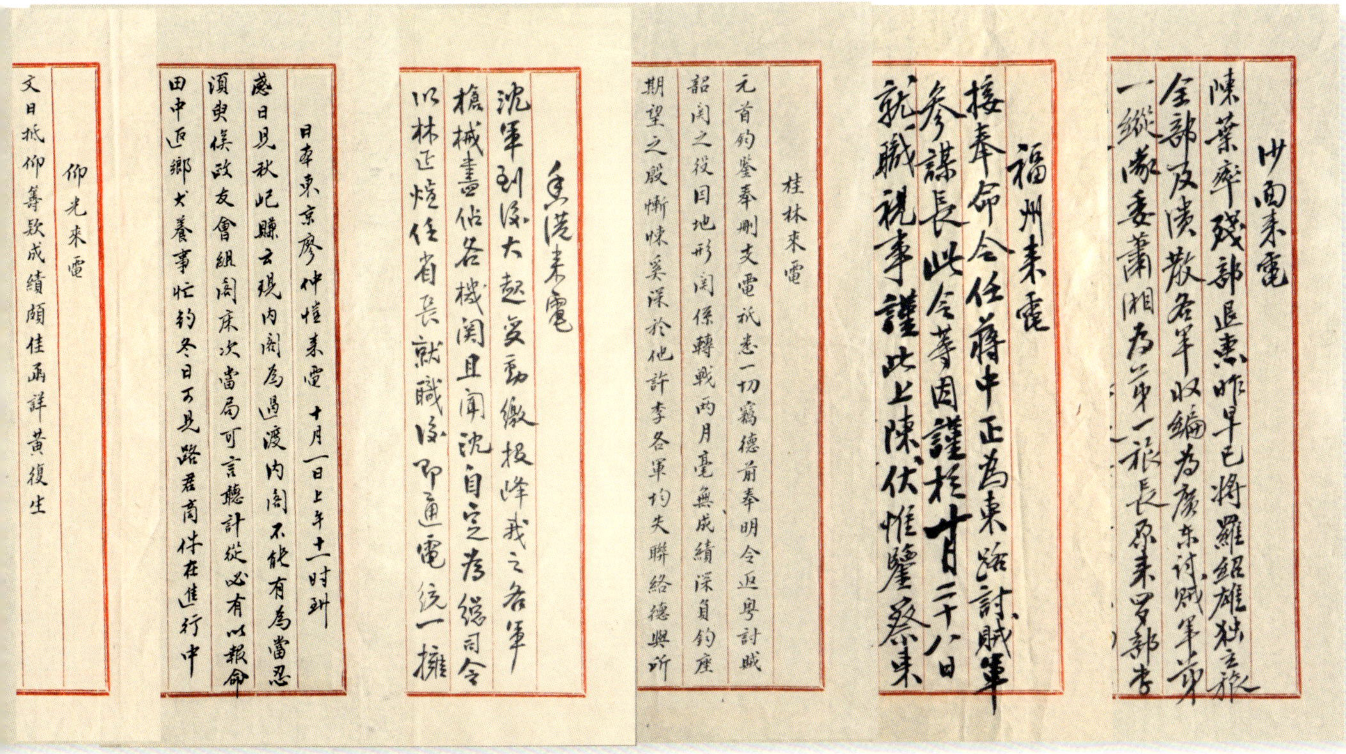

沙面來電

陳葉率殘部退惠，昨早已將羅紹雄狀玄旅全部及潰散各軍收編為廣東討賊軍第一縱隊，委蕭湘為第一旅長，原來羅部者

福州來電

接奉命令任蔣中正為東路討賊軍參謀長，此令等因，謹於十月二十八日就職視事，謹此上陳，伏惟鑒察來

桂林來電

元首鈞鑒：奉删支電，祗悉一切。竊德前奉明令返粵討賊，韶關之役因地形關係，轉戰兩月，毫無成績，深負鈞座期望之殷，慚悚奚深。於他許李各軍均失聯絡，德與所

香港來電

沈軍到後，大起發動，繳抵降我之各軍槍械，盡佔各機關，且聞沈自定為總司令，以林近煌任省長，就職後即通電統一擁

日本東京廖仲愷來電　十月一日上午十一時到

慈日見秋屺賺云：現內閣為過渡內閣，不能有為，當忍須臾。俟政友會組閣，床次當局，可言聽計從，必有以報命。田中近鄉，犬養事忙，約冬日可見。路君商件在進行中

仰光來電

文日抵仰，籌款成績頗佳，函詳。黃復生

交部三軍政部四財政部五農礦
部六工商部七教育部八交通部
二十一憲法未頒布以前各院長皆歸總
統任免而督率之
二十二憲法草案當本於建國大綱及訓
政憲政兩時期之成績由立法院議
訂隨時宣傳於民衆以備到時採
擇施行
二十三全國有過半數省分達至憲政
開始時期即全省之地方自治完
全成立時期則開國民大會決定
憲法而頒布之
二十四憲法頒布之後中央統治權則歸
於國民大會行使之即國民大會
對於中央政府官員有選舉權有
罷免權對於中央法案有創制權
有複決權
二十五憲法頒布之日即為憲政告成
之時而全國國民則依憲法行全
國大選舉國民政府則於選舉
完畢之後三個月解職而授政於民
選之政府是為建國之大功告成
民國十三年四月初二日寫於廣州大
本營為
賢妻慶齡玩索 孫文

1924 年 4 月 2 日孙中山书赠宋庆龄的《国民政府建国大纲》册页

A copy of *the Fundamental of National Reconstruction of the Nationalist Government* written by Dr. Sun Yat-sen ,which was presented to Soong Ching Ling on April 2, 1924.

● 1924 年 1 月 20 日，中国国民党第一次全国代表大会召开当天，通过了孙中山交由临时中央执行委员会提出的《组织国民政府之必要提案》，提案内含孙中山手拟的《国民政府建国大纲》全文 25 条。《国民政府建国大纲》是孙中山对未来中华民国政治制度设想的纲领性文件，可分为两部分。第一部分，孙中山对其三民主义思想，即“民生”“民权”“民族”的主张进行了阐述；第二部分，孙中山阐述了其“革命程序论”，即“军政”“训政”“宪政”。4 月 2 日，孙中山在广州陆海军大元帅大本营手书《国民政府建国大纲》全文，落款处题有“为贤妻庆龄玩索”字样。

工商事業本縣之資力不能發展
與興辦而須賴外資乃能經營者
當由中央政府為之協助而所獲之
純利中央與地方政府各占其半

十三各縣對於中央政府之負担當以每
縣之歲收百分之幾為中央歲費每
年由國民代表定之其限度不得少
於百分之十不得加於百分之五十

十四每縣地方自治政府成立之後得選
國民代表一員以組織代表會參預
中央政事

十五凡候選及任命人員無論中央與地
方皆須經中央考試銓定資格者
乃可

十六凡一省全數之縣皆達完全自治
者則為憲政開始時期國民代表會得
選舉省長為本省自治之監督
至於該省內之國家行政則省長
受中央之指揮

十七在此時期中央與省之權限採均
權制度凡事務有全國一致之性
質者劃歸中央有因地制宜之
性質者劃歸地方不偏於中央集
權或地方分權

十八縣為自治之單位省立於中央與
縣之間以收聯絡之效

十九在憲開始時期中央政府當完成
設立五院以試行五權之治其序
列如下曰行政院曰立法院曰司法
院曰考試院曰監察院

二十行政院暫設如下各部一內政部二外

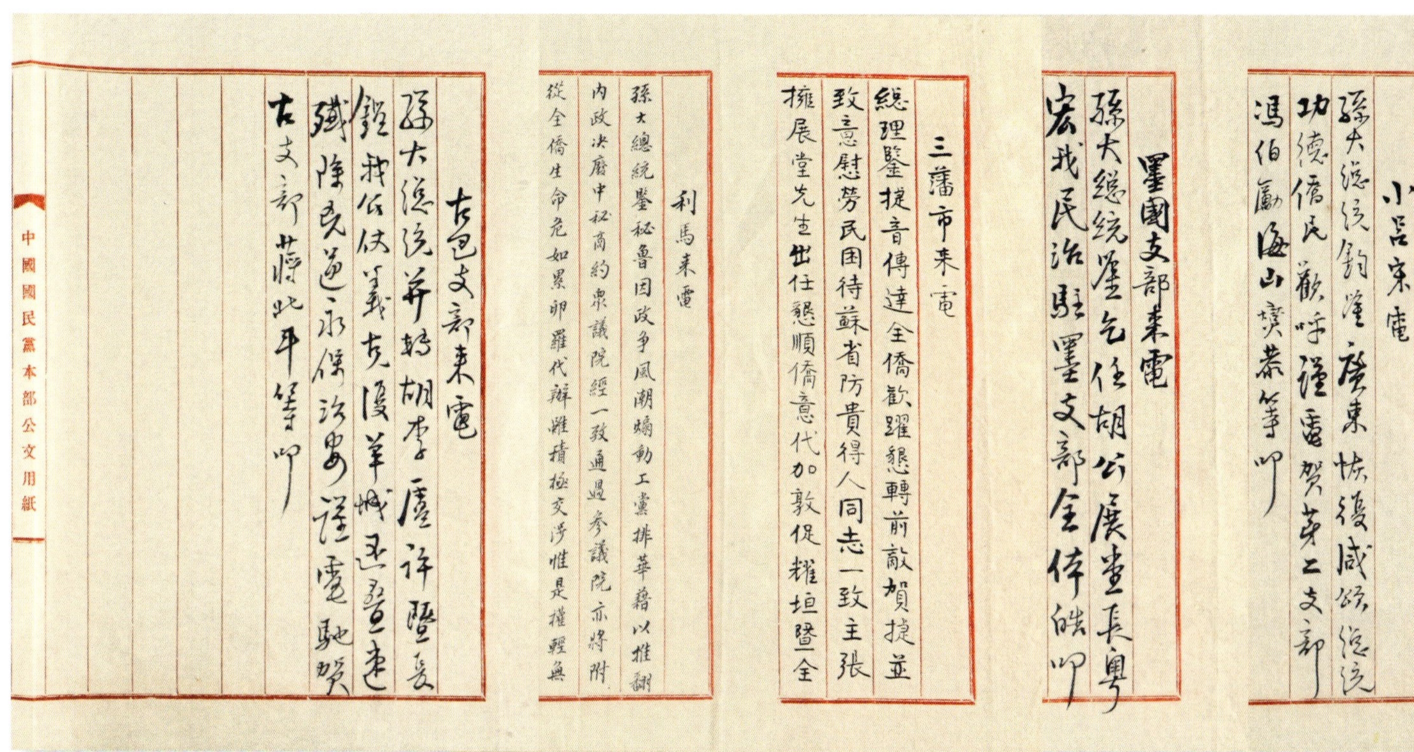

宋庆龄协助孙中山处理的各地函电

Correspondence and telegrams handled by Dr. Sun Yat-Sen with Soong Ching Ling 's assistance

● 1922 年至 1923 年孙中山在沪期间，宋庆龄协助他处理各地函电，这些函电来自广州、桂林、福州、香港、北京，以及日本、美国、墨西哥等地，达数百封之多。

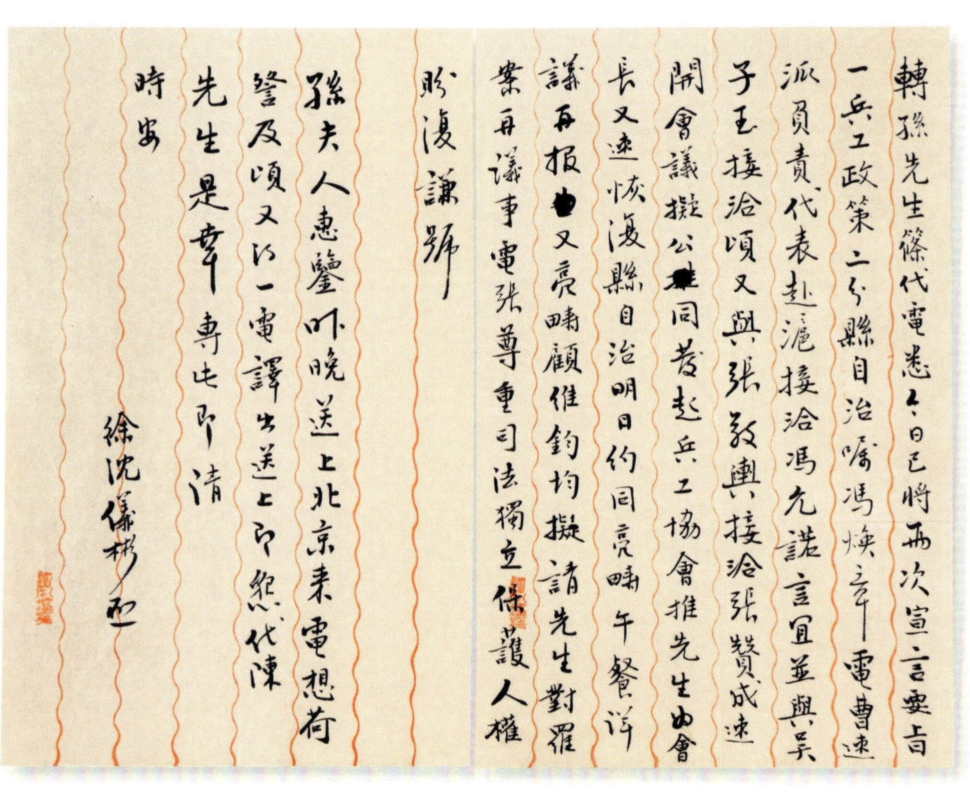

轉孫先生篠代電悉五日已將兩次宣言要旨
一兵工政策二分縣自治囑馮煥章一電曹速
派員負責代表赴滬接洽馮允諾言宜並與吳
子玉接洽頃又與張敬輿接洽張贊成速
開會議擬公推同孝赴兵工協會推先生由會
長又速恢復縣自治明日約同亮疇午餐詳
議再報又亮疇顧維鈞均擬請先生對羅
案再議事電張尊重司法獨立保護人權
肸復 謙歸

孫夫人惠鑒 昨晚送上北京來電想荷
詧及 頃又得一電譯出送上即煩代陳
先生是荷 專此即請
時安
徐沈儀彬

徐沈仪彬致宋庆龄函

Correspondence to Soong Ching Ling from Xu-Shen Yibin

●徐沈仪彬在致宋庆龄函中，恳请她向孙中山代陈新译出的徐谦致孙中山电，徐沈仪彬为徐谦夫人。推测此电发出时间为1923年1月20日，是宋庆龄帮助孙中山处理往来函电的直接史证。

考試合格之員到各縣協助人民籌備自治其程度以全縣人口調查清楚全縣土地測量完竣全縣警衛辦理妥善四境縱橫之道路修築成功而其人民曾受四權使用之訓練而完畢其國民之義務誓行革命之主義者得選舉縣官以執行一縣之政事得選舉議員以議立一縣之法律始成為一完全自治之縣

九 一完全自治之縣其國民有直接選舉官員之權有直接罷免官員之權有直接創制法律之權有直接複決法案之權

十 每縣開創自治之時必須先規定全縣私有土地之價其法由地主自報之地方政府則照價徵稅並可隨時照價收買自此次報價之後若土地因政治之改良社會之進步而增價者則其利益當為全縣人民所共享而原主不得而私之

十一 土地之歲收地價之增益公地之生產山林川澤之息鑛產水力之利皆為地方政府之所有而用以經營地方人民之事業及育幼養老濟貧救災醫病與夫種種公共之需

十二 各縣之天然富源與及大規模之

國民政府建國大綱

一　國民政府本革命之三民主義五權憲法以建設中華民國

二　建設之首要在民生故對於全國人民之食衣住行四大需要政府當與人民協力共謀農業之發展以足民食共謀織造之發展以裕民衣建築大計畫之各式屋舍以樂民居修治道路運河以利民行

三　其次為民權故對於人民之政治知識能力政府當訓導之以行使其選舉權行使其罷官權行使其創制權行使其複決權

四　其三為民族故對於國內之弱小民族政府當扶植之使之能自決自治對於國外之侵畧強權政府當抵禦之並同時修改各國條約以恢復我國際平等國家獨立

五　建設之程序分為三期一曰軍政時期二曰訓政時期三曰憲政時期

六　在軍政時期一切制度悉隸於軍政之下政府一面用兵力以掃除國內之障礙一面宣傳主義以開化全國之人心而促進國家之統一

七　凡一省完全底定之日則為訓政開

宋庆龄保存的孙中山记事本

Dr. Sun Yat-sen's notebook preserved by Soong Ching Ling

●这本宋庆龄保存的记事本为黑色硬皮封面，钤“孙宋庆龄”印。内有孙中山书信两封和文稿两篇，按先后顺序分别为孙中山 1923 年 7 月 26 日致徐谦函，孙中山为谢彬《新疆游记》所作序言，孙中山 1923 年 7 月 4 日致徐谦函，孙中山著《民族主义》自序。

孙中山在 1923 年 7 月致徐谦的两封信中，对徐谦以委员制建立政府的提议表示反对，主张以革命的方式解决中国时局问题。

孙中山在 1920 年 7 月为谢彬《新疆游记》所作序言中，盛赞其“行路四万六千余里，载三十万言”的非凡之举，并劝勉“有志之士，当立心做大事，不可立心做大官”。此书为 1916 年至 1917 年谢彬以财政部特派员身份赴新疆阿尔泰地区历经 15 个月的考察后形成的调查日记汇编。

孙中山于 1924 年 3 月在广州陆海军大元帅大本营为《民族主义》所作序言中，介绍自己的著作《国家建设》一书内含八册，其中《民族主义》一册本已脱稿，但毁于陈炯明叛变。中国国民党第一次全国代表大会召开后，孙中山将 1924 年在国立广东大学和国立广东高等师范学校所作的演讲讲义修改印行为单行本《民族主义》，以宣传“三民主义之奥义、五权宪法之要旨”。

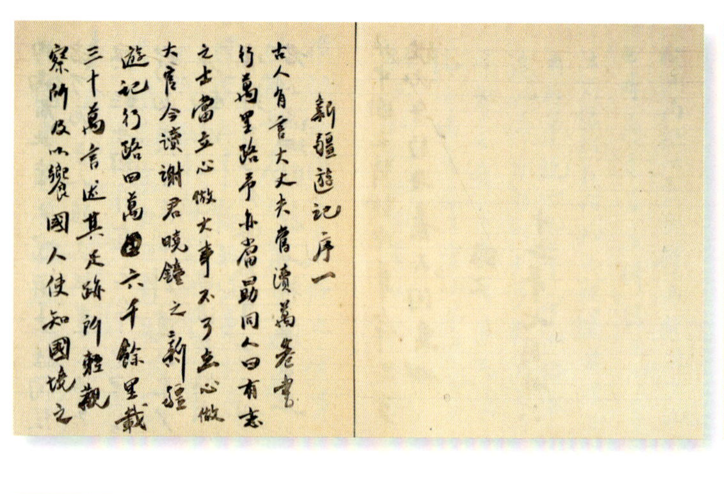
新疆遊記序一

古人有言大丈夫當讀萬卷書行萬里路予亦嘗勗同人曰有志之士當立心做大事不可立心做大官今讀謝君曉鐘之新疆遊記行路四萬六千餘里載三十萬言述其足跡所經觀察所及以饗國人使知國境之

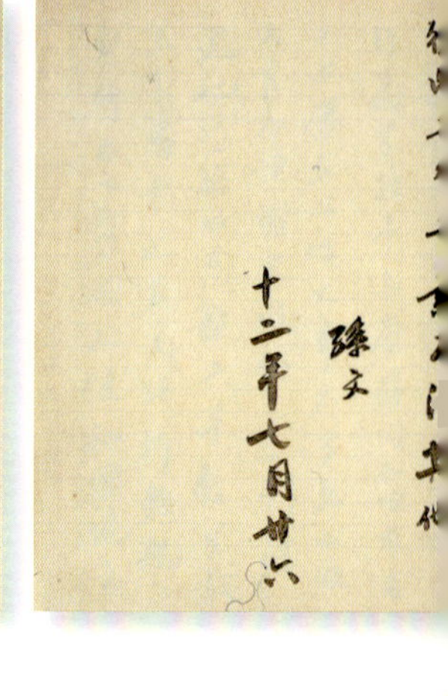
孫文

十二年七月廿六

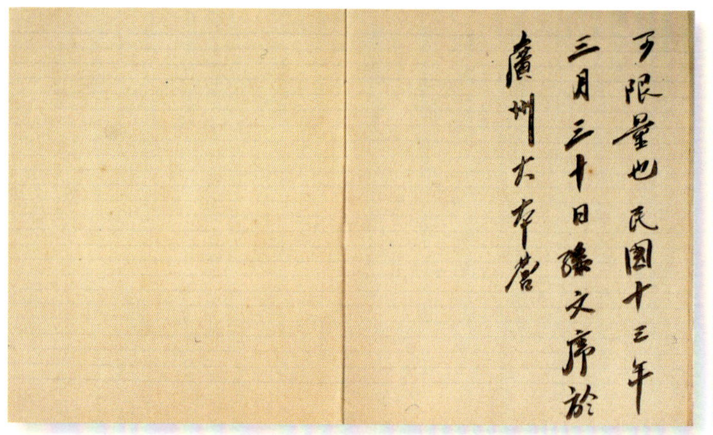
可限量也 民國十三年三月三十日孫文序於廣州大本營

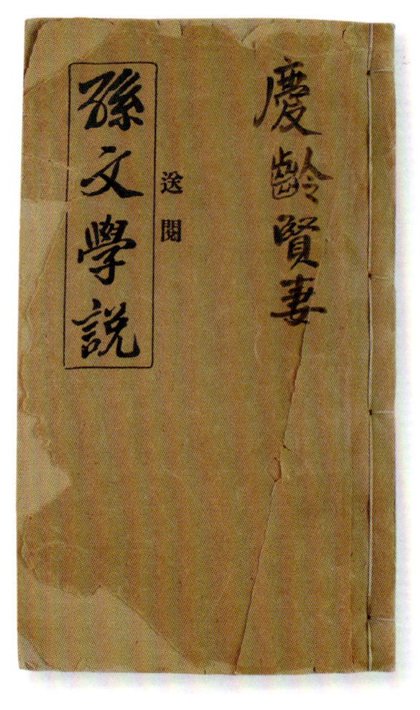

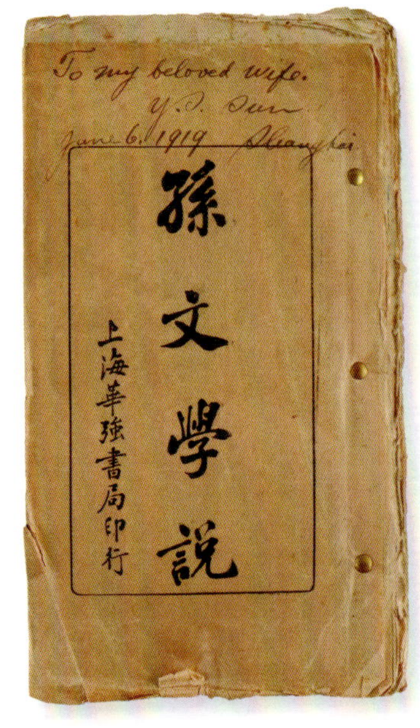

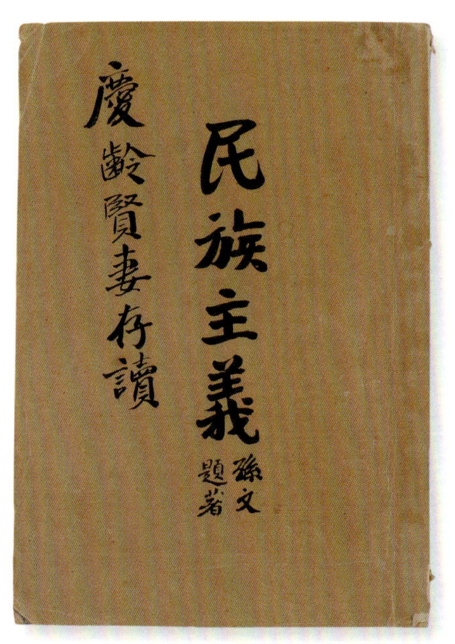

孙中山题赠宋庆龄的《孙文学说》和《民族主义》

Complimentary copies of *The Doctrine of Sun Wen* and *The Principle of Nationalism* presented to Soong Ching Ling by Dr. Sun Yat-sen

---

● 1918 年，在宋庆龄的帮助下，屡受挫折的孙中山在上海寓所潜心著述《孙文学说》，系统阐释“知难行易”的哲学思想。《孙文学说》曾先印刷“送阅本”供孙中山赠送他人之用，此件送阅本上有孙中山题写的“庆龄贤妻”字样。另一件《孙文学说》为 1919 年上海华强书局的印本，上有孙中山题写的“To my beloved wife”（给我亲爱的妻子）字样。

为宣传中国国民党第一次全国代表大会所确定的政策,1924 年 1 月 27 日至 8 月 30 日，孙中山先后 16 次到国立广东大学(含到国立广东高等师范学校的 2 次)礼堂向干部和师生系统讲述三民主义，并以此讲义为基础修改编印《民族主义》一书。此件《民族主义》上有孙中山题写的“庆龄贤妻存读”字样。

孙中山穿过的长衫

A long gown worn by Dr. Sun Yat-sen

●此件为宋庆龄保存的孙中山穿过的长衫，青灰色，圆形立领，大襟右衽，左右开裾。这件长衫为平面式裁剪，是孙中山习惯穿着的便服。

孙中山的遮阳帽和手杖

Sunhat and walking stick used by Dr. Sun Yat-sen

●孙中山外出视察或督战时经常头戴遮阳帽，手拄手杖。孙中山使用过的此件遮阳帽由上海华球帽厂生产，是民国时期流行的巴拿马式样。孙中山使用过的手杖为六边形柱体，杖脚及杖头包银。

孙中山的手枪

Pistol used by Dr. Sun Yat-sen

●孙中山一生为革命奔波，身历险境，出生入死，此件手枪是孙中山当年护卫防身之用，为美国制造的柯尔特转轮手枪，枪管口径为0.38英寸（9毫米），弹容6发。

孙中山名片印版

The card of copper used by Dr. Sun Yat-sen

●此件为宋庆龄保存的孙中山名片印版，铜质，凹版，由怡顺公司制造，上有孙中山英文名字"SUN YAT-SEN"的反向图像。

“中华革命党本部之印”印章

Seal of *the Headquarter of the Chinese Revolutionary Party*

● 1913 年 7 月，孙中山发动反对袁世凯的二次革命，失败后再次避走日本。孙中山痛感国民党组织松散，缺乏战斗力，遂对国民党进行整顿。1914 年 7 月 8 日，孙中山在东京建立中华革命党，并担任该党总理。中华革命党本部为该党的领导中枢，本部会议由总理及各部部长、总理秘书组织，决定党的革命方略。此印即由本部使用。在孙中山的领导下，中华革命党人在多省发动起义，开展反袁斗争。1919 年 10 月 10 日，中华革命党改组为中国国民党，“中华革命党本部之印”遂不用。

“中华民国陆海军大元帅之印”印章

Seal of *the Generalissimo of the Navy and Army of the Republic of China*

● 1921 年 12 月，孙中山抵达广西桂林，组建北伐大本营，整军北伐。1922 年 3 月因入湘受阻而班师回粤。同年 6 月陈炯明在广州发动武装叛乱，孙中山被迫离粤，大本营解散。1923 年 1 月陈炯明被逐出广州，孙中山于同年 3 月 2 日在广州重建陆海军大元帅大本营，本人担任大本营最高职务中华民国陆海军大元帅。此印系孙中山所使用，孙中山以大元帅名义发布的命令、宣告、布告常钤此印。从《陆海军大元帅大本营公报》所载的孙中山发布的各种政令看，此印从 1924 年 1 月 2 日启用，1925 年 3 月孙中山逝世，此印即不再使用，由宋庆龄收藏。1925 年 7 月，中华民国国民政府在广州成立，陆海军大元帅大本营结束。

“孙文之印 逸仙长寿”对印

Twin seals of *Sun Wen's Seal* and *Long Life for Yat-sen*

●此对印刻于 1916 年。孙中山 1922 年至 1923 年期间使用此印较多，且主要用于题词，如孙中山 1922 年手书“博爱”横幅。篆刻者陈融为中国同盟会会员，曾任广州国民政府秘书长。边款为“民国五年十二月陈融谨篆”、“颙厂”（陈融的号）。

“孙文藏书”印章

Seal of *Sun Wen Book Collection*

●孙中山一生酷爱读书，他的革命思想的形成和发展与他精心研读大量中西文书籍有着极为密切的关系。在孙中山和宋庆龄上海莫利爱路寓所内，保存有五千余册不同语种的藏书。孙中山读书甚少做眉批，但有在部分藏书上署名和钤印的习惯。此印为胡汉民的堂弟胡毅生刻制后赠与孙中山，孙中山的部分藏书上钤有此印。边款为“中山先生命刻 毅生谨篆”。

胡毅生（1883—1957），广东番禺（今广州）人。1903 年东渡日本留学，后加入兴中会，是中国同盟会最早的会员之一。1914 年加入中华革命党，参与二次革命和护法之役。1939 年后历任国民政府委员、总统府顾问等职。1957 年在台北病逝。

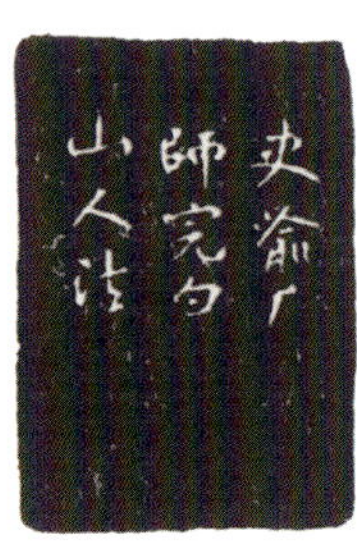

“孙宋庆龄 琼英”对印

Twin seals of *Sun Soong Ching Ling* and *Qiongying*

●此对印为史喻厂1927年刻制后赠与宋庆龄，宋庆龄的部分藏书钤有此印。“琼英”为宋庆龄早年使用的化名。边款为“丁卯七月喻厂仿汉”和“史喻厂师完白山人法”。完白山人即清代著名篆刻家、书法家邓石如。史喻厂名谦，号喻厂，为国民党党员。辛亥武昌首义，曾任江宁县知县。后隐身上海，以卖文鬻书自给。他的书法和篆刻为孙中山所欣赏，曾为孙中山及其他国民党人士刻制印章。

1913 年日本神户有志欢迎会赠孙中山的银瓶

Silver vase presented to Dr. Sun Yat-sen by a group in Kobe, Japan

● 1913 年 2 月 11 日，孙中山以筹办全国铁路的名义赴日本考察。3 月 13 日，孙中山抵达神户，受到当地华侨和支持他革命的部分日本政界人士的欢迎，神户有志欢迎会将此银瓶赠送给孙中山。

一旦我们所爱的人与我们诀别而去，那么相互爱得越深，我们所承受的悲痛也就更深沉……但正像你所说，我们终有甜蜜和爱恋的记忆留在心间。

——1975 年宋庆龄致廖梦醒信

The more we have loved each other, the deeper our grief becomes once our loved ones are forever gone··· But as you said, we are lucky to have sweets and loving memories in our hearts.

——Soong Ching Ling to Liao Mengxing in 1975

宋庆龄保存的孙中山安葬纪念章

A commemorative badge marking Dr. Sun Yat-sen's burial preserved by Soong Ching Ling

● 1929 年 6 月 1 日，国民政府在南京为孙中山举行奉安大典，此件为奉安大典定制的纪念品。孙中山安葬纪念章为总理奉安委员会在美国定制，共两万枚，铜质，分发给参加奉安大典的来宾。纪念章正面为孙中山浮雕头像，背面铸孙中山陵寝图案，并刻有“孙中山先生安葬纪念　中华民国十八年三月十二日”。奉安大典原定孙中山逝世纪念日（3 月 12 日）举行，因迎榇大道未能按时完工，延至 6 月 1 日举行，而纪念章已在美国提前定制，故日期仍为 3 月 12 日。纪念章侧面铸有制造公司的名称“纽约奖章艺术公司”和纪念章编号。宋庆龄收藏的此枚孙中山安葬纪念章编号为 6364。

宋庆龄保存的孙中山安葬纪念瓷瓶和笔筒

A porcelain bottle and a pen vase marking Dr. Sun Yat-sen's burial preserved by Soong Ching Ling

● 1929 年中央陶瓷厂为孙中山奉安而烧制的瓷瓶和笔筒，图案分别为龙纹和松柏仙鹤纹，底款印有“总理奉安纪念 中央陶瓷厂制”字样。

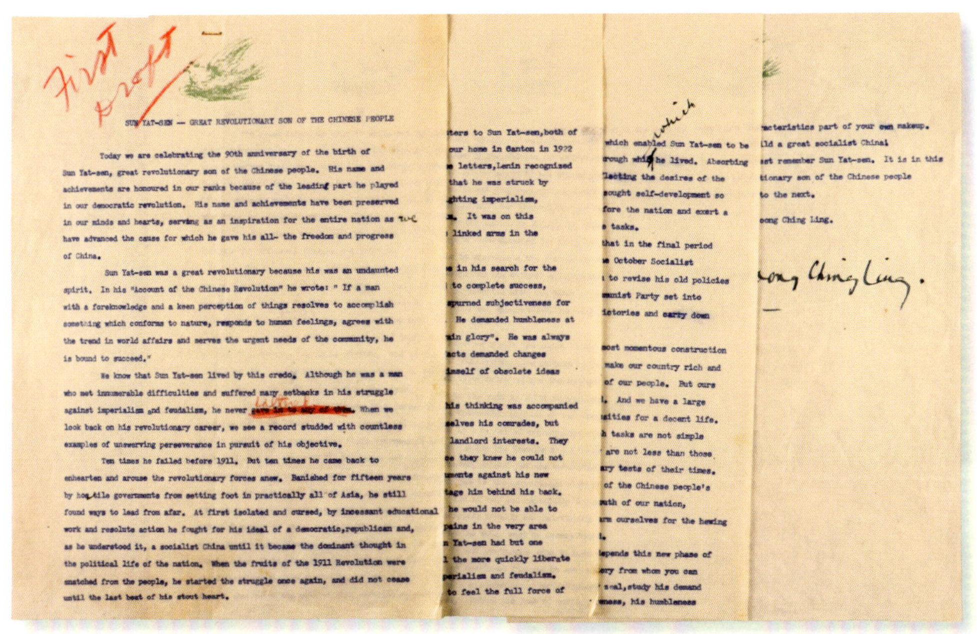

First Draft

SUN YAT-SEN — GREAT REVOLUTIONARY SON OF THE CHINESE PEOPLE

Today we are celebrating the 90th anniversary of the birth of Sun Yat-sen, great revolutionary son of the Chinese people. His name and achievements are honoured in our ranks because of the leading part he played in our democratic revolution. His name and achievements have been preserved in our minds and hearts, serving as an inspiration for the entire nation as we have advanced the cause for which he gave his all- the freedom and progress of China.

Sun Yat-sen was a great revolutionary because his was an undaunted spirit. In his "Account of the Chinese Revolution" he wrote: " If a man with a foreknowledge and a keen perception of things resolves to accomplish something which conforms to nature, responds to human feelings, agrees with the trend in world affairs and serves the urgent needs of the community, he is bound to succeed."

We know that Sun Yat-sen lived by this credo. Although he was a man who met innumerable difficulties and suffered many setbacks in his struggle against imperialism and feudalism, he never ~~gave in to any of them~~. When we look back on his revolutionary career, we see a record studded with countless examples of unswerving perseverance in pursuit of his objective.

Ten times he failed before 1911. But ten times he came back to enhearten and arouse the revolutionary forces anew. Banished for fifteen years by hostile governments from setting foot in practically all of Asia, he still found ways to lead from afar. At first isolated and cursed, by incessant educational work and resolute action he fought for his ideal of a democratic,republican and, as he understood it, a socialist China until it became the dominant thought in the political life of the nation. When the fruits of the 1911 Revolution were snatched from the people, he started the struggle once again, and did not cease until the last beat of his stout heart.

1956 年 11 月宋庆龄纪念孙中山诞辰九十周年文稿《孙中山——中国人民伟大的革命的儿子》

The article *Sun Yat-sen—Great Revolutionary Son of the Chinese People* Soong Ching Ling wrote in November 1956, on the occasion of the 90th anniversary of Dr. Sun Yat-sen's birth

● 1956 年 11 月，为纪念孙中山诞辰九十周年，宋庆龄撰写《孙中山——中国人民伟大的革命的儿子》一文，后公开发表在 11 月 4 日的《人民日报》上。此件是宋庆龄撰写的英文底稿，文首有宋庆龄标注的“First Draft”（初稿）字样，文稿中文发表版增加了大量有关孙中山生平的内容。文稿点明了孙中山的毕生追求是中国的自由和进步，简要回顾了孙中山的革命历程，着重论述了他大无畏、坚韧不移和自我革新的精神，指出年轻人应向孙中山学习，把孙中山的精神遗产世代流传下去。文稿有多处宋庆龄修改的痕迹，最后一页有宋庆龄英文签名。

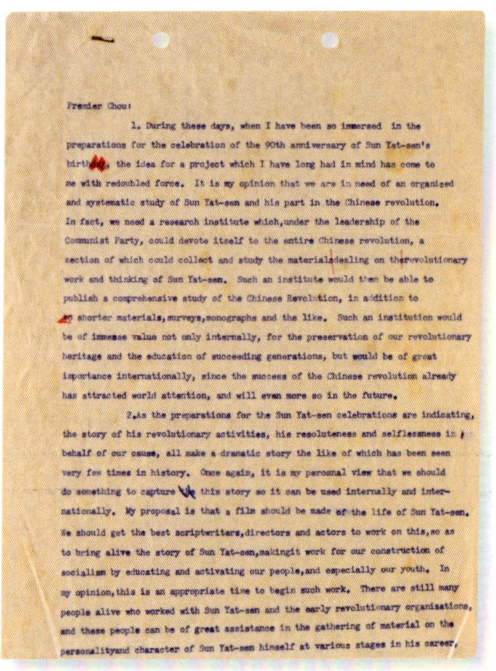

Premier Chou:

1. During these days, when I have been so immersed in the preparations for the celebration of the 90th anniversary of Sun Yat-sen's birthday, the idea for a project which I have long had in mind has come to me with redoubled force. It is my opinion that we are in need of an organised and systematic study of Sun Yat-sen and his part in the Chinese revolution. In fact, we need a research institute which, under the leadership of the Communist Party, could devote itself to the entire Chinese revolution, a section of which could collect and study the materials dealing on the revolutionary work and thinking of Sun Yat-sen. Such an institute would then be able to publish a comprehensive study of the Chinese Revolution, in addition to to shorter materials, surveys, monographs and the like. Such an institution would be of immesse value not only internally, for the preservation of our revolutionary heritage and the education of succeeding generations, but would be of great importance internationally, since the success of the Chinese revolution already has attracted world attention, and will even more so in the future.

2. As the preparations for the Sun Yat-sen celebrations are indicating, the story of his revolutionary activities, his resoluteness and selflessness in behalf of our cause, all make a dramatic story the like of which has been seen very few times in history. Once again, it is my perosnal view that we should do something to capture this story so it can be used internally and internationally. My proposal is that a film should be made of the life of Sun Yat-sen. We should get the best scriptwriters, directors and actors to work on this, so as to bring alive the story of Sun Yat-sen, makingit work for our construction of socialism by educating and activating our people, and especially our youth. In my opinion, this is an appropriate time to begin such work. There are still many people alive who worked with Sun Yat-sen and the early revolutionary organizations, and these people can be of great assistance in the gathering of material on the personalityand character of Sun Yat-sen himself at various stages in his career,

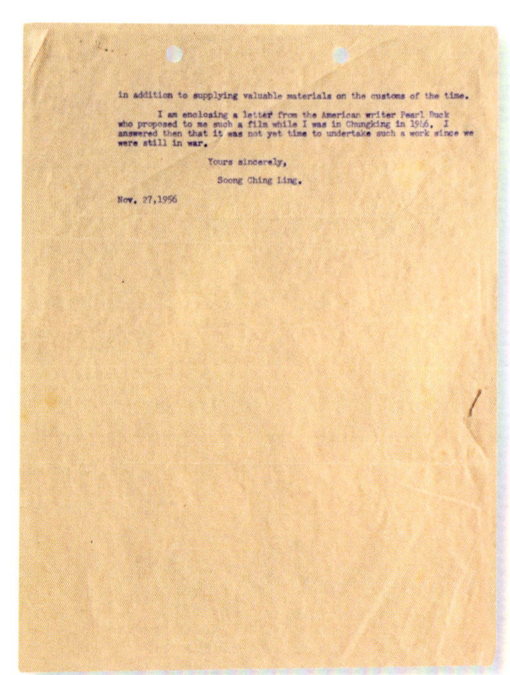

in addition to supplying valuable materials on the customs of the time.

I am enclosing a letter from the American writer Pearl Buck who proposed to me such a film while I was in Chungking in 1946. I answered then that it was not yet time to undertake such a work since we were still in war.

Yours sincerely,

Soong Ching Ling.

Nov. 27, 1956

1956 年 11 月 27 日宋庆龄致周恩来信

A letter to Zhou Enlai from Soong Ching Ling on November 27, 1956

● 1956 年 11 月，宋庆龄在筹备孙中山诞辰九十周年纪念时，考虑应该对孙中山一生的事业和他在中国革命史上的地位加以有组织的研究，因此于 11 月 27 日专门致信周恩来提出建议。信中写道，我们需要建立一个研究所，在中国共产党领导下专门整理和分析中国革命史料，包括孙中山的革命事迹和思想，并建议将孙中山的事迹编制成电影来进行宣传。

1966 年 12 月中华书局发行的《孙中山选集》

Selected Works of Sun Yat-sen published by Zhonghua Book Company in December 1966

●为纪念孙中山诞辰一百周年，1966 年 12 月，中华书局重印了 1956 年人民出版社出版、宋庆龄题写书名的《孙中山选集》。此件《孙中山选集》为精装本，书外壳有红色护封，上面横书金色的“孙中山选集 宋庆龄题”字样。

全國人民代表大會常務委員會

Sun Yat-sen: Resolute and Persistent Revolutionary

On this special occasion to commemorate the One Hundredth Anniversary of Sun Yat-sen's birth, I should like to share with you my thoughts about the life and activities of this great son of our people.

He was born before imperialism, before the monopoly capital began to dominate the world. He came to the world when the dynastic power in our country had just been badly shaken by the Tai Ping Peasant Uprising, and our people had just started to contact the capitalistic nations.

He died at the time when the imperialist power was about at its zenith. Not only the European powers were contemplating to divide our territory, but nearby Japanese militarism already threatened our entire nation, which was then broken up into several parts

1966 年宋庆龄纪念孙中山诞辰一百周年英文原稿《孙中山——坚定不移、百折不挠的革命家》

Manuscript of Soong Ching Ling's article *Sun Yat-sen: Resolute and Persistent Revolutionary* in 1966, on the occasion of the 100th anniversary of Dr. Sun Yat-sen's birth

● 1966 年 11 月 12 日，首都各界在人民大会堂隆重集会，纪念孙中山诞辰一百周年。宋庆龄在会上以《孙中山——坚定不移、百折不挠的革命家》为题作了长篇发言，回忆了孙中山一生的革命历程，指出：“孙中山是一个有远大目光和深刻预见的人。因此，他的一生是一个顽强的革命者的一生。他一开始就不相信封建王朝，而随着革命的发展，他对人民则产生越来越大的信心。”“孙中山一生奋斗的目标已经实现并且已经超过了。但他的名字和他的精神仍然活在我们心中。”本文为宋庆龄为大会发言准备的文稿，共 51 页，为目前所见最长的宋庆龄英文手稿。宋庆龄为准备此稿花费很长时间，并请好友伊斯雷尔·爱泼斯坦润色，最后在大会上的中文发言稿经周恩来审定过。

...sant
The
...ople
...er
...an
later
were
path
attend
...ly
...arning
...ebrood

ough separated
, his mind
know his
thinking had
he felt
ntry was the
nasch. In
rm to serve
revolutionary
gan: Divine
f organizing
ed that as

irectly or
sover, mono
us. A dis
the imperialist
taken place
ip of the Chinese
have removed
feudal rule
. Not only
ocratic revo
lliant achievements
ople are solidly
nization and
se of the
rialism regime
political and

Sun Yat-sen
memory
nary who was
revolution.
d vision and
s life was
ed not be a
. He never
the Chinese
gly reposed
corrupted
the people
mind to

ntemporaries
Yen Fu (嚴複),
al characters
in the people
tary and the
as a constitu-
even joined
Manchu
ut sixty years
re the Chinese
platform for
ut world, he
must be done
real and true
le, why not
ould to the

complete?"
ge to declare
t our people
as Japan.
. Reformists
people would
est, and would
est. Before
eformists
t one time
...) It
ecision, their
ck of sympathy
repressive
sion and
carrying out

volutionary
at all.
wholeheartedly
e in holding
g before he
Yat-sen,
Comrade
eningrad,
3 about
guard Asia"
, Chinese
Sun Yat-sen
t, Lenin
the Chinese
at time.

ary correctly.
uggle.
when I
d (in 1916 in
f buildings
e! In the
but now
es belonging
Each of these
itory, except
gambling,
kind of
d enjoy
is why
ter hunger

othing.
is declining
being con-
. It is
"
;
in tour
province,
He told his
n is to enable
sionals to
s provincial
re the master.
ne who
Chen-wu
properties

othing.
is declining
being con-
. It is
"
;
in tour
province,
He told his
n is to enable
sionals to
s provincial
re the master.
ne who
Chen-wu
properties

现在，我认为我们背弃了孙中山领导群众和加强群众的政策，因此我只有暂时引退以待更贤明的政策出现。我对于革命并没有灰心。使我失望的，只是有些领导过革命的人已经走上了歧途。

——1927 年宋庆龄文稿《为抗议违反孙中山的革命原则和政策的声明》

At the moment I feel that we are turning aside from Dr. Sun's policy of leading and strengthening the people. Therefore, I must withdraw until wiser policies prevail. There is no despair in my heart for the revolution, my disheartenment is only for the path into which some of those who have been leading the revolution have strayed.

——*Statement Issued in Protest Against the Violation of Sun Yat-sen's Revolutionary Principles and Policies* by Soong Ching Ling in 1927

宋庆龄旅居欧洲时的留影

Soong Ching Ling in Europe

●大革命失败后，1927年8月，宋庆龄赴苏联寻求中国革命的出路。1928年5月至1931年8月，宋庆龄旅居德国柏林（1929年5月至9月曾因参加孙中山奉安大典短暂回国）。在欧洲，宋庆龄潜心研读孙中山的著作及马克思、恩格斯、列宁的经典著作和左派报刊，后期还扩大了和德国进步人士的联系，推动了她追求社会进步和向共产主义者的转变。图为宋庆龄旅居欧洲时的留影。

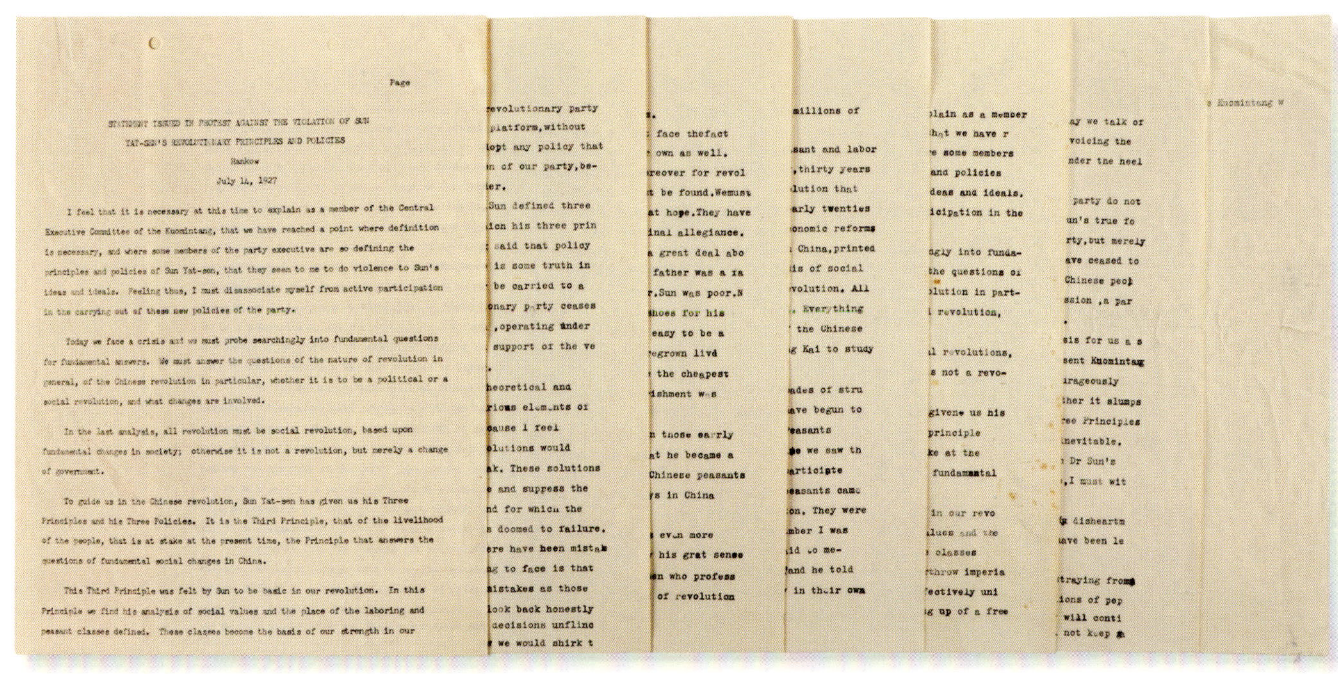

Page

STATEMENT ISSUED IN PROTEST AGAINST THE VIOLATION OF SUN YAT-SEN'S REVOLUTIONARY PRINCIPLES AND POLICIES

Hankow

July 14, 1927

I feel that it is necessary at this time to explain as a member of the Central Executive Committee of the Kuomintang, that we have reached a point where definition is necessary, and where some members of the party executive are so defining the principles and policies of Sun Yat-sen, that they seem to me to do violence to Sun's ideas and ideals. Feeling thus, I must disassociate myself from active participation in the carrying out of these new policies of the party.

Today we face a crisis and we must probe searchingly into fundamental questions for fundamental answers. We must answer the questions of the nature of revolution in general, of the Chinese revolution in particular, whether it is to be a political or a social revolution, and what changes are involved.

In the last analysis, all revolution must be social revolution, based upon fundamental changes in society; otherwise it is not a revolution, but merely a change of government.

To guide us in the Chinese revolution, Sun Yat-sen has given us his Three Principles and his Three Policies. It is the Third Principle, that of the livelihood of the people, that is at stake at the present time, the Principle that answers the questions of fundamental social changes in China.

This Third Principle was felt by Sun to be basic in our revolution. In this Principle we find his analysis of social values and the place of the laboring and peasant classes defined. These classes become the basis of our strength in our

1927 年 7 月宋庆龄文稿《为抗议违反孙中山的革命原则和政策的声明》

Statement Issued in Protest Against the Violation of Sun Yat-sen's Revolutionary Principles and Policies drafted by Soong Ching Ling in July 1927

● 1927 年，蒋介石集团、汪精卫集团先后在上海和武汉发动反革命政变。7 月 14 日，宋庆龄拒绝出席汪精卫召开的“分共”会议，并于当天撰写《为抗议违反孙中山的革命原则和政策的声明》，指出：“孙中山的政策是明明白白的。如果党内领袖不能贯彻他的政策，他们便不再是孙中山的真实信徒；党也就不再是革命的党，而不过是这个或那个军阀的工具而已。”宣布“暂时引退以待更贤明的政策出现”，与蒋介石、汪精卫控制的国民党断绝关系。7 月 17 日，宋庆龄出走上海。次日，该声明在汉口《英文中央日报》刊登。该报被查封后，中文译稿以《孙宋庆龄对时局宣言》为题被印成传单在武汉张贴，表达了宋庆龄维护孙中山新三民主义和三大政策的坚定立场，在国际国内产生了强烈反响。

1927年9月7日宋庆龄到达莫斯科火车站时留影

A photo showing Soong Ching Ling on her arrival at Moscow Railway Station on September 7, 1927

●为了寻求中国革命的出路，实现孙中山访问莫斯科的遗愿，宋庆龄决定秘密出访苏联。1927年8月22日，宋庆龄从上海启程赴莫斯科。图为宋庆龄9月7日抵达莫斯科火车站时受到苏联政府代表和数千名各界群众的热烈欢迎。

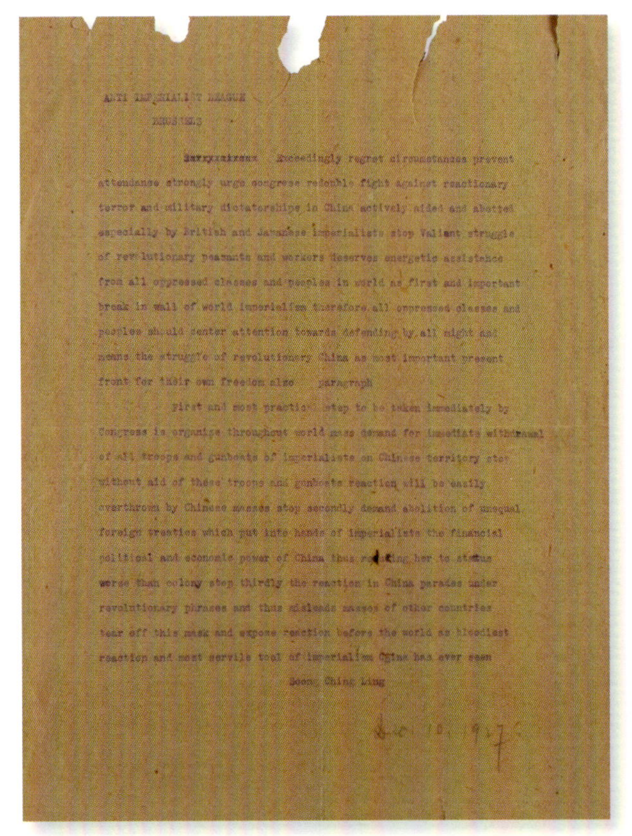

ANTI IMPERIALIST LEAGUE
BRUSSELS

Exceedingly regret circumstances prevent attendance strongly urge congress redouble fight against reactionary terror and military dictatorships in China actively aided and abetted especially by British and Japanese imperialists stop Valiant struggle of revolutionary peasants and workers deserves energetic assistance from all oppressed classes and peoples in world as first and important break in wall of world imperialism therefore all oppressed classes and peoples should center attention towards defending by all might and means the struggle of revolutionary China as most important present front for their own freedom also paragraph

First and most practical step to be taken immediately by Congress is organise throughout world mass demand for immediate withdrawal of all troops and gunboats of imperialists on Chinese territory stop without aid of these troops and gunboats reaction will be easily overthrown by Chinese masses stop secondly demand abolition of unequal foreign treaties which put into hands of imperialists the financial political and economic power of China thus reducing her to status worse than colony stop thirdly the reaction in China parades under revolutionary phrases and thus misleads masses of other countries tear off this mask and expose reaction before the world as bloodiest reaction and most servile tool of imperialism China has ever seen

Soong Ching Ling

Dec 10, 1927

1927 年 12 月 10 日宋庆龄致反帝大同盟的电报稿

Soong Ching Ling's telegram of December 10, 1927 to the Anti-Imperialist League

●反帝大同盟，1927 年 2 月在比利时首都布鲁塞尔创办。布鲁塞尔会议选举巴比塞、爱因斯坦、宋庆龄等人组成反帝大同盟名誉主席团。1927 年 12 月 10 日，反帝大同盟执行理事会在布鲁塞尔举行，当时正在莫斯科的宋庆龄致电该会，对因故未能参会表示遗憾，希望大会支持中国革命，与中国在英、日帝国主义的帮助和怂恿下的反动恐怖和军事独裁政权作斗争。电报右下方为宋庆龄标注的日期“Dec 10, 1927”（1927 年 12 月 10 日）。

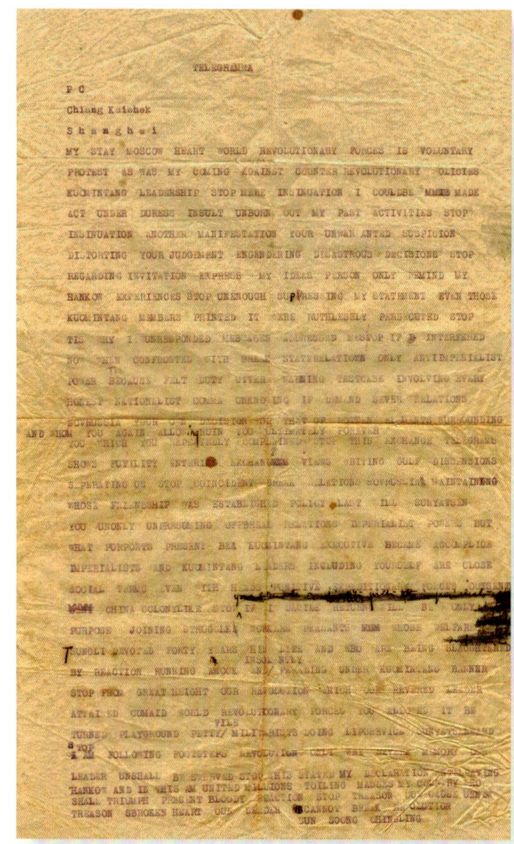

TELEGRAMMA

P C

Chiang Kaishek

Shanghai

MY STAY MOSCOW HEART WORLD REVOLUTIONARY FORCES IS VOLUNTARY PROTEST AS WAS MY COMING AGAINST COUNTER REVOLUTIONARY POLICIES KUOMINTANG LEADERSHIP STOP HERE INSINUATION I COULDBE MADE ACT UNDER DURESS INSULT UNBORN OUT MY PAST ACTIVITIES STOP INSINUATION ANOTHER MANIFESTATION YOUR UNWARRANTED SUSPICION DISTORTING YOUR JUDGEMENT ENGENDERING DISASTROUS DECISIONS STOP REGARDING INVITATION EXPRESS MY IDEAS PERSON ONLY REMIND MY HANKOW EXPERIENCES STOP [illegible] SUPPRESSING MY STATEMENT EVEN THOSE KUOMINTANG MEMBERS PRINTED IT WERE RUTHLESSLY PERSECUTED STOP [illegible]

1927年12月23日宋庆龄致蒋介石电报稿

Soong Ching Ling's telegram of December 23, 1927 to Chiang Kai-shek

● 1927年12月11日，中国共产党在广州发动起义，建立广州苏维埃政府，被国民党反动派镇压。南京国民政府以广州起义受苏联领事馆煽动为由，派兵围攻广州苏联领事馆，并与苏联断交。正在莫斯科访问的宋庆龄先后两次致电蒋介石，对他的行为表示抗议。此件12月23日宋庆龄致蒋介石电，驳斥其所说的她留在莫斯科是受人胁迫这一说法，申明：“我留在世界革命力量的心脏莫斯科是自愿的，就如同我的访问是一种对国民党领导人的反革命的自愿的抗议一样。”表示：“我将踏着革命者的足迹继续前进，这是缅怀我们领袖的唯一道路，我在这条道路上将绝不回头。”电报有多处修改痕迹。

Légation
de la
République Chinoise

N° 845.

Passeport
(Diplomatique)

Nous Envoyé Extraordinaire et Ministre Plénipotentiaire de Chine en France etc. etc.
Prions les Autorités Civiles et Militaires des Puissances Amies, de vouloir bien laisser passer librement Mademoiselle C.L. SOUN, Délégué du Gouvernement National de la République Chinoise

qui se rend en Allemagne et retour

et lui accorder aide et protection en cas de besoin.

Donné à Paris le 29 Octobre 1929.

POUR LE MINISTRE
ET PAR AUTORISATION

LÉGATION DE LA RÉPUBLIQUE DE CHINE EN FRANCE

Valable pour

1929 年宋庆龄赴欧洲的护照

Soong Ching Ling's passport to Europe in 1929

● 1929 年 5 月宋庆龄因参加孙中山奉安大典短暂回国，9 月再次赴欧游历。此件为 1929 年 10 月 29 日中华民国驻法兰西公使馆发给宋庆龄的赴德国等欧洲国家的护照，护照上照片为 1927 年宋庆龄在武汉留影。

1933 年宋庆龄与中国民权保障同盟部分成员合影

Soong Ching Ling with some members of the China League for Civil Rights in 1933

●大革命失败后，国民党制造白色恐怖，共产党人和革命群众惨遭屠杀。1932 年 12 月宋庆龄在上海发起组织中国民权保障同盟，任同盟主席，积极援助营救遭拘禁的革命者和爱国志士。图为宋庆龄与中国民权保障同盟部分成员合影，照片贴于卡纸之上，卡纸下部宋庆龄写有“The Civil Rights League 1933，Hu Yuetse, Lin Yutang, Lee Pei-hwa, Yang Chien, Soong Ching Ling”（中国民权保障同盟，1933 年，胡愈之，林语堂，黎沛华，杨铨，宋庆龄）。杨铨即杨杏佛。

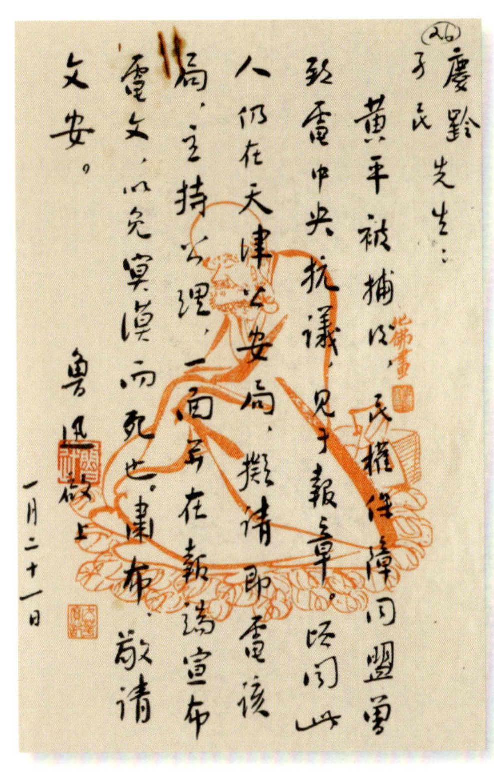
慶齡
子民 先生：
黃平被捕後，民權保障同盟曾致電中央抗議，見于報章，昨聞此人仍在天津公安局，擬請即電該局，主持公理，一面並在報端宣布電文，以免冥漠而死也。敬請
文安。
魯迅 敬上
一月二十一日

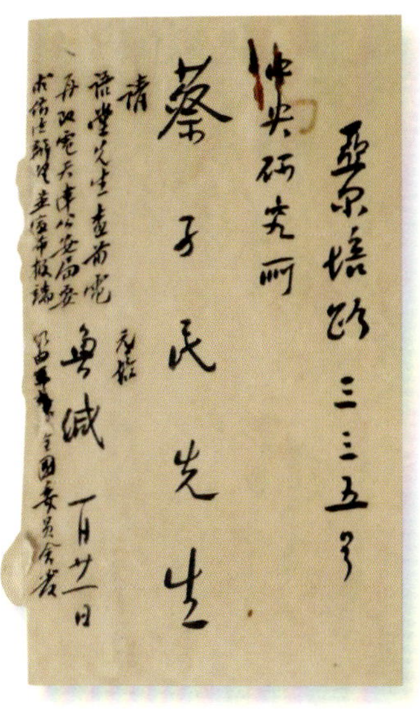
亞爾培路三三五號
中央研究院
蔡子民先生
魯緘 一月廿一日

1933 年 1 月 21 日鲁迅致宋庆龄、蔡元培信

Lu Xun's letter of January 21, 1933 to Soong Ching Ling and Cai Yuanpei

● 1933 年 1 月 21 日，为营救中共临时中央政治局成员黄平，中国民权保障同盟上海分会执行委员鲁迅致函宋庆龄和蔡元培（字子民），请他们即电关押黄平的天津公安局，“主持公理”，并请在报端宣布电文，“以免冥漠而死也”。宋庆龄与蔡元培接信后，立即采取措施组织营救。蔡元培时任中国民权保障同盟副主席。

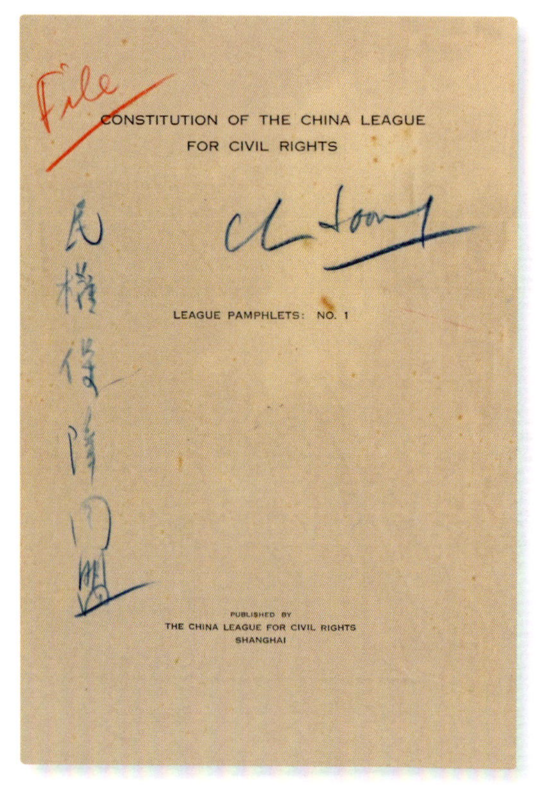

《中国民权保障同盟章程》

Constitution of the China League for Civil Rights

●《中国民权保障同盟章程》阐明同盟的目的是释放国内政治犯，废除对他们的非法拘禁、酷刑及杀戮；为国内政治犯提供法律及其他援助；争取人民的出版、言论、集会和结社自由。《章程》封面有宋庆龄书写的“民权保障同盟”，“C L Soong”（宋庆龄）和“File”（存档）字样。

“中国民权保障同盟主席之印”印章

Soong Ching Ling's Seal of *the President of the China League for Civil Rights*

●此件为宋庆龄担任中国民权保障同盟主席时使用的印章，牛角制作，以篆书刻制。

1936年宋庆龄在上海莫利爱路寓所与牛兰之子吉梅合影

Soong Ching Ling with Jimmy in her residence on Rue Molière, Shanghai in 1936

● 1931年6月15日，泛太平洋产业同盟上海办事处秘书（实为共产国际执行委员会国际联络部组织科负责人）牛兰及其夫人被公共租界巡捕房拘捕，后引渡给国民党当局以“共产党嫌疑”的罪名关押在南京监狱。中共上海党组织、苏联情报部门及宋庆龄、杨杏佛等各界进步人士多方营救，并由宋庆龄任主席组成上海牛兰夫妇营救委员会，与国际援救牛兰委员会合作，为争取释放牛兰夫妇而斗争。宋庆龄一度将牛兰的儿子吉梅接到家中照顾，图为1936年宋庆龄在上海莫利爱路寓所阳台与吉梅合影。

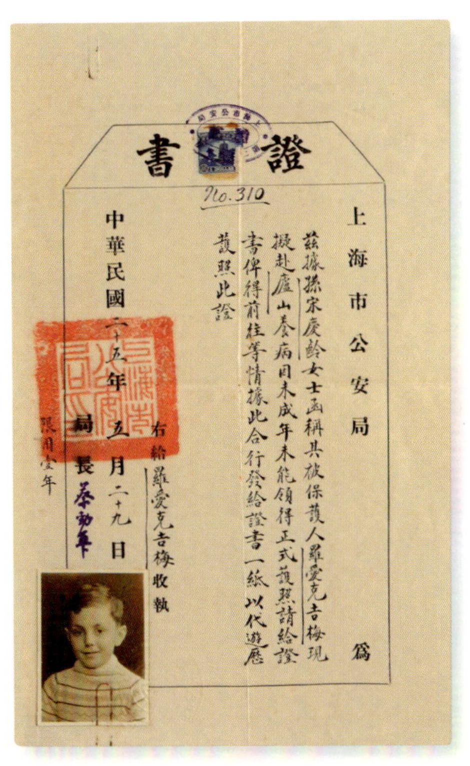

證書

No.310

上海市公安局　爲

茲據孫宋慶齡女士函稱其被保護人羅愛克吉梅現擬赴廬山養病因未成年未能領得正式護照請給證書俾得前往等情據此合行發給證書一紙以代遊歷護照此證

右給羅愛克吉梅收執

中華民國二十五年五月二十九日

局長蔡勁軍

限用壹年

1936 年宋庆龄请上海市公安局为牛兰之子吉梅出具的身份证书

The identity certificate for Jimmy issued by Shanghai Public Security Bureau, according to Soong Ching Ling's request in 1936

● 1936 年 5 月 29 日上海市公安局为宋庆龄所照顾的牛兰之子吉梅出具到庐山养病的证书，以代替吉梅因未成年而没有领到的正式护照。

我坚决相信，中国不但能够抵抗日本的任何侵略，并且能够而且必须准备收复失地。中国最大的力量在于中国人民大众已经觉醒起来了。

——1937 年宋庆龄文稿《中国是不可征服的》

It is my confident belief that China not only can resist every and any Japanese aggression but that she can and must prepare to recover her lost territories. China's greatest strength lies in the awakening of her masses.

——*China Unconquerable* by Soong Ching Ling in 1937

1932 年宋庆龄在上海真如前线留影

A photo of Soong Ching Ling at the battlefield of Zhenru County

● 1932 年 1 月 28 日，日本军队入侵上海，淞沪抗战爆发。2 月 6 日，宋庆龄到真如前线慰问抗战将士，她手持未爆炸的炸弹在残垣断壁前留影，表明抗战到底的决心。

“国民伤兵医院理事会”印章

Seal of *International Hospital for Chinese Wounded Soldiers*

● 1932年一·二八淞沪抗战爆发后，宋庆龄积极支援十九路军抗战，多次亲临前线慰问，并倡议筹备建立伤兵医院。3月5日，国立交通大学（上海本部）校长黎照寰应宋庆龄之请，将交大条件最好的执信西斋腾空供伤兵医院用，建立一所拥有300张病床的“国民伤兵医院”，宋庆龄亲任医院理事主管医院事务。此件为当时国民伤兵医院理事会使用的公章。4月中旬，国民伤兵医院完成使命宣告结束。

1932 年宋庆龄与南洋广肇义学童子军团在国民伤兵医院合影

Soong Ching Ling with the Boy Scouts of Nanyang Guangzhao Free School at International Hospital for Chinese Wounded Soldiers in 1932

●国民伤兵医院建立后，由交大附小学生组成的南洋广肇义学童子军团曾在该院服务，图为宋庆龄与他们的合影。

宋庆龄为国民伤兵医院的伤兵播放唱片

Soong Ching Ling played music record to pacify the wounded soldiers of International Hospital for Chinese Wounded Soldiers

● 1932 年一·二八淞沪抗战期间，抵御日寇的十九路军多为广东人，宋庆龄（右一）为国民伤兵医院的伤兵专门购置了广东音乐唱片并为其播放，希望通过乡音抚慰伤兵们的思乡之情，右二为秘书黎沛华。右图为宋庆龄保存的广东音乐唱片《秋水龙吟》。

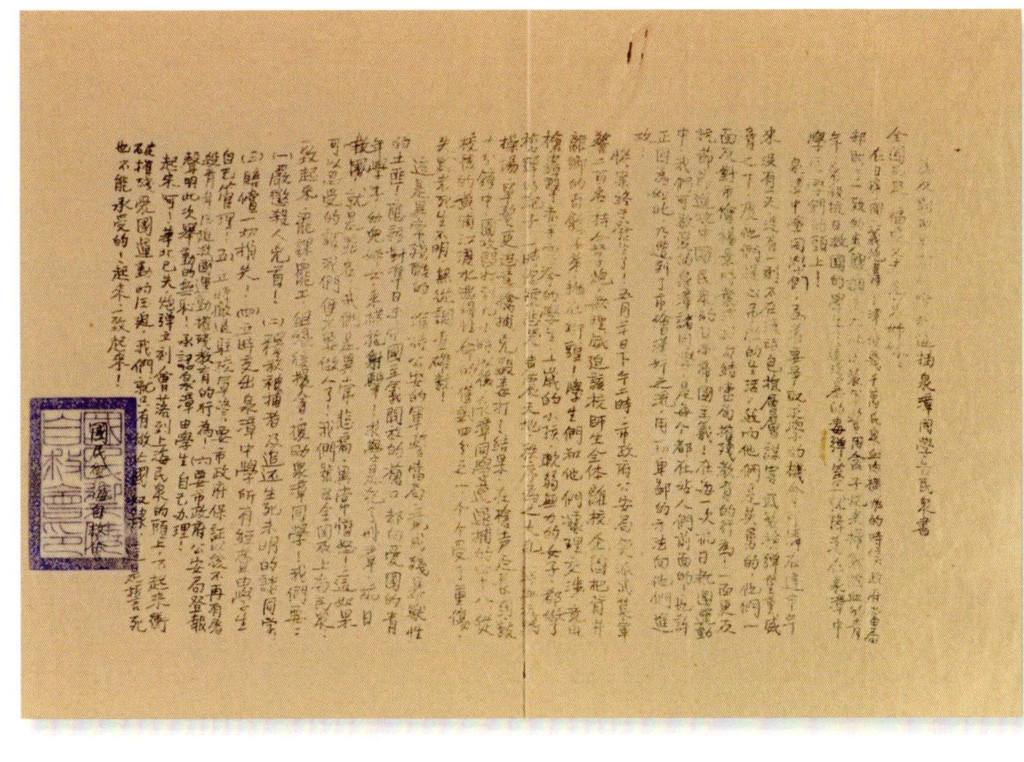

国民御侮自救会传单

A leaflet issued by the National Salvation Organization

●为推动国民党统治区的抗日救亡运动，宋庆龄领导的中国民权保障同盟，与中国共产党协商后决定发起成立范围更广泛的抗日救亡团体——国民御侮自救会。1933 年 3 月 8 日，中国民权保障同盟上海分会和上海工人界、学生界、文化界等 28 个团体在八仙桥青年会举行国民御侮自救会成立大会。宋庆龄当选为该会主席，号召全国抗日群众团结抵抗日本帝国主义的侵略。此件传单名称为《为反对政府当局惨杀逮捕泉漳同学告民众书》，谴责 1933 年 5 月 20 日国民党当局在日本帝国主义侵略中国的危急关头，枪击逮捕上海泉漳中学的爱国青年学生，提出“严惩杀人凶手”“释放被捕者”等六项主张。

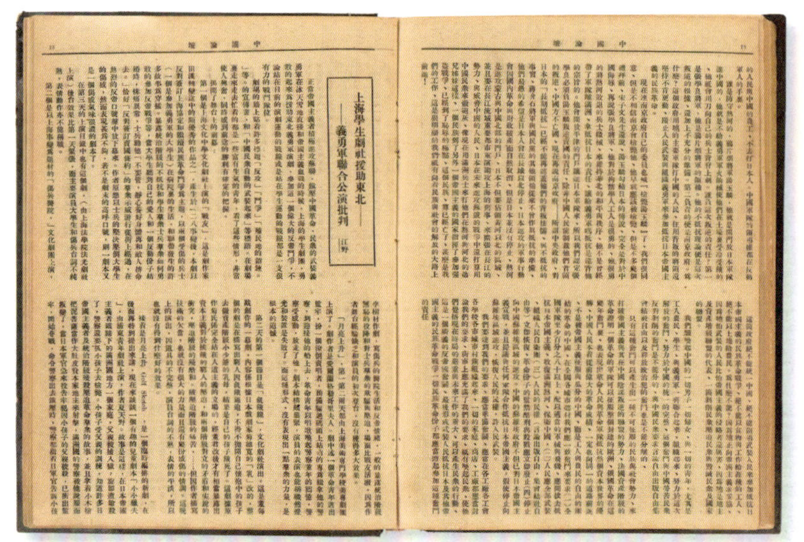

上海學生劇社援助東北義勇軍聯合公演批判

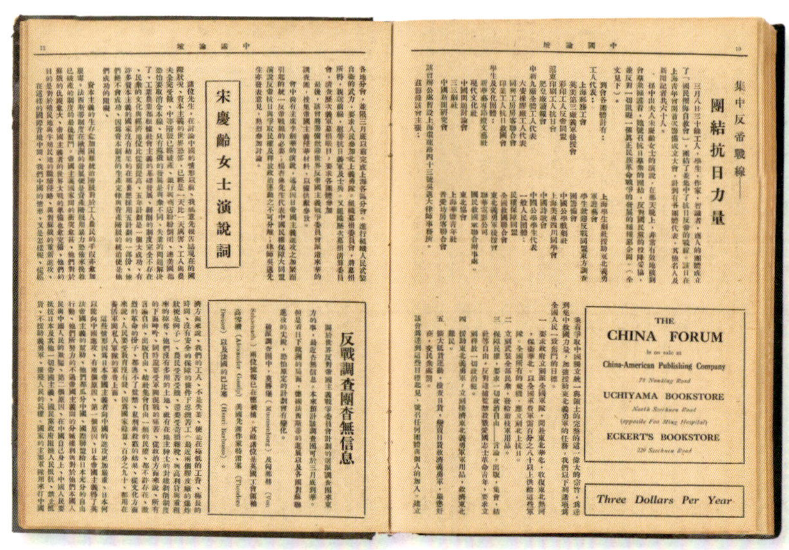

宋慶齡女士演說詞

反戰調查團杳無信息

集中反帝戰線——團結抗日力量

THE CHINA FORUM

China-American Publishing Company

UCHIYAMA BOOKSTORE

ECKERT'S BOOKSTORE

Three Dollars Per Year

《中国论坛》刊载宋庆龄在国民御侮自救会成立大会上的演说词

The China Forum published Soong Ching Ling's speech on the inaugural meeting of the National Salvation Organization

● 1933 年 3 月，《中国论坛》刊登了宋庆龄在国民御侮自救会成立大会上的演说词。宋庆龄在演说中第一次阐明她对中国抗战的全面主张，提出反对国民党的妥协投降政策，要求停止向苏维埃区域的进攻，全国抗日群众紧密团结，共同抗击日本帝国主义的侵略等。

1938 年保卫中国同盟中央委员会部分成员在香港合影

Soong Ching Ling with some members of the Central Committee of the China Defence League in Hong Kong in 1938

● 1937 年 11 月，日军占领上海。12 月 23 日，宋庆龄接受中共中央建议，离沪赴港。1938 年 6 月，在周恩来的建议下，宋庆龄在香港成立保卫中国同盟，以宣传抗战、争取外援为宗旨。保卫中国同盟将援助重点放在共产党领导的抗日根据地和敌后游击区。图为 1938 年宋庆龄与保卫中国同盟中央委员会部分成员在香港合影。左起：爱泼斯坦、邓文钊、廖梦醒、宋庆龄、希尔达·塞尔温-克拉克、诺曼·法朗士、廖承志。

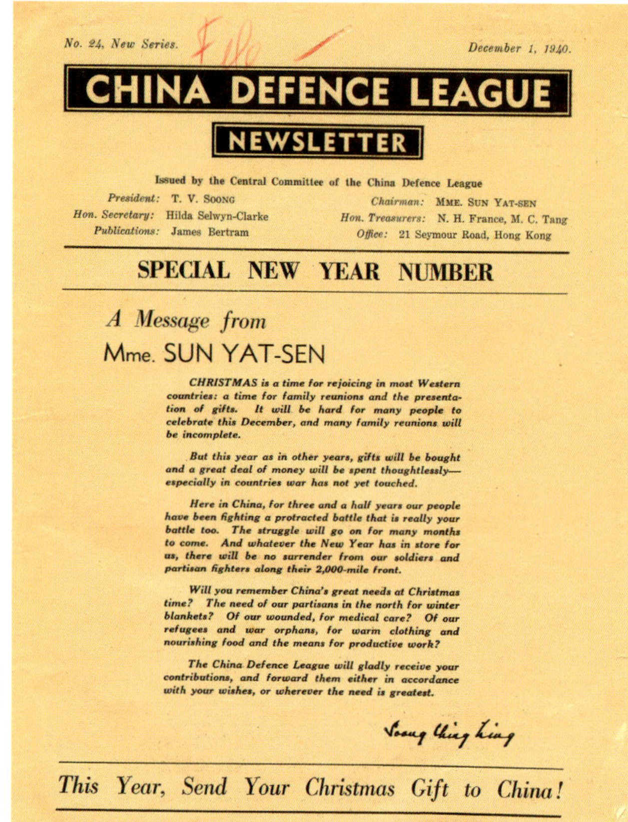

No. 24, New Series. December 1, 1940.

CHINA DEFENCE LEAGUE

NEWSLETTER

Issued by the Central Committee of the China Defence League

President: T. V. Soong *Chairman:* Mme. Sun Yat-sen
Hon. Secretary: Hilda Selwyn-Clarke *Hon. Treasurers:* N. H. France, M. C. Tang
Publications: James Bertram *Office:* 21 Seymour Road, Hong Kong

SPECIAL NEW YEAR NUMBER

A Message from Mme. SUN YAT-SEN

CHRISTMAS is a time for rejoicing in most Western countries: a time for family reunions and the presentation of gifts. It will be hard for many people to celebrate this December, and many family reunions will be incomplete.

But this year as in other years, gifts will be bought and a great deal of money will be spent thoughtlessly—especially in countries war has not yet touched.

Here in China, for three and a half years our people have been fighting a protracted battle that is really your battle too. The struggle will go on for many months to come. And whatever the New Year has in store for us, there will be no surrender from our soldiers and partisan fighters along their 2,000-mile front.

Will you remember China's great needs at Christmas time? The need of our partisans in the north for winter blankets? Of our wounded, for medical care? Of our refugees and war orphans, for warm clothing and nourishing food and the means for productive work?

The China Defence League will gladly receive your contributions, and forward them either in accordance with your wishes, or wherever the need is greatest.

Soong Ching Ling

This Year, Send Your Christmas Gift to China!

《保卫中国同盟新闻通讯》（1940 年 12 月 1 日，第 24 期）

The issue of *China Defence League Newsletter*（December 1,1940, No.24）

●《保卫中国同盟新闻通讯》是 1938 年初夏保卫中国同盟发行的英文双周刊，旨在向海外宣传中国抗战的真实情况，争取国际援助。此期新闻通讯为 1940 年 12 月 1 日出版的贺岁专号，刊载了宋庆龄呼吁海外援助的来信、白求恩写给国外朋友的信（节选）及白求恩逝世一周年纪念文章等，重点说明共产党所在的抗日根据地和游击区各种物资匮乏的客观情况。

保卫中国同盟 1943 年年报《在中国游击区》

A report titled *In Guerrilla China* issued by the China Defence League in 1943

● 1939 年保卫中国同盟用英文编撰出版了第一本年度工作报告，向海外援华团体及有关人士通报保卫中国同盟的工作，以后每年编撰一本。这本《在中国游击区》是 1943 年保卫中国同盟年报，介绍了保卫中国同盟援助的抗日根据地医疗服务(国际和平医院、医学训练、医药生产等)、难民救济工作、西北边区的工业合作社、边区的儿童工作以及广州国际医疗服务队。1943 年年报编撰时，保卫中国同盟办事处已迁至重庆，年报由美国援华会帮助在纽约出版。保卫中国同盟 1943 年年报介绍的都是抗日游击区的各项工作，因此《在中国游击区》就成了这份年报的标题。年报扉页钤“宋庆龄”印。

宋庆龄的“SCL”印章金戒指

Gold ring seal of “SCL” (abbreviation of Soong Ching Ling)

●戒面 SCL 为宋庆龄英文名字 Soong Ching Ling 的缩写。宋庆龄在香港募捐时，常用此印章戒指在捐助者的收据上盖章并签名。

宋庆龄保存的唱片专辑《起来——新中国之歌》

The record album of *Chee Lai: Songs of New China* preserved by Soong Ching Ling

---

● 1941 年，积极倡导民众歌咏运动的刘良模邀请美国著名歌唱家保罗·罗伯逊与美国华裔青年歌咏团录制以《起来》为名的唱片专辑。唱片由美国主旨唱片公司（Keynote Recordings）1941 年录制发行，内含 3 张 72 转黑胶唱片。唱片共 7 首中国特色的民谣和革命歌曲，其中保罗·罗伯逊用中英文演唱了《起来》《凤阳歌》等 4 首歌曲，刘良模指挥美国华裔青年歌咏团用中文演唱了《锄头歌》《军民合作》等 3 首歌曲。宋庆龄专门为唱片作序，时在美国的林语堂亦为唱片作序。唱片发行的收益捐赠给保卫中国同盟支援中国抗战。

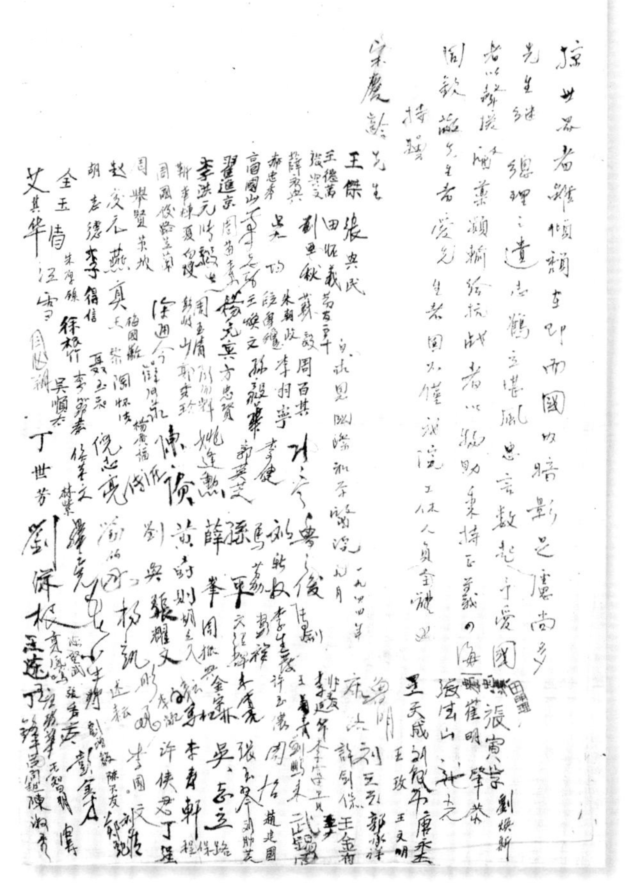

1944 年延安白求恩国际和平医院全体工休人员联名签署的致宋庆龄感谢信

A joint letter of thanks to Soong Ching Ling from the whole staff of Bethune International Peace Hospital in Yan'an in 1944

●抗战期间，宋庆龄募集大量物资支援敌后根据地的国际和平医院。1944 年 9 月，刘伯承、陈赓等 140 余名延安白求恩国际和平医院的休养人员和工作人员，集体签名致函宋庆龄，感谢她长期以来的支持和帮助。致敬书称：“掠世界者虽倾颓在即，而国内暗影足虑尚多。先生继总理之遗志，鹤立堪风，忠言数起，予爱国者以声援。医药频输，给抗战者以物助。秉持正义，四海同钦。敬先生者，爱先生者，固不仅我院工休人员全体也。持赠宋庆龄先生。”

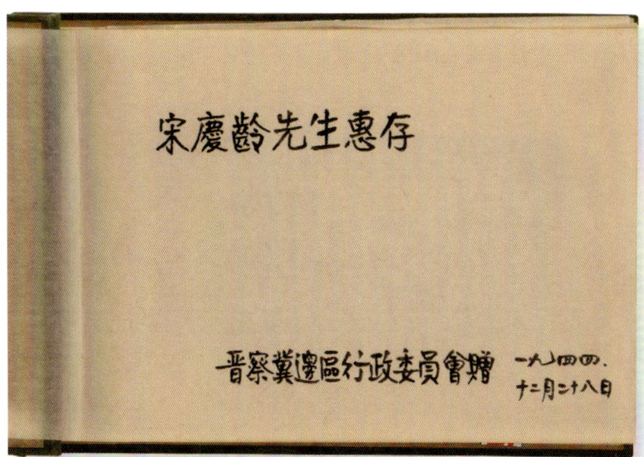

1944 年晋察冀边区行政委员会赠送宋庆龄的边区票样册

A complete set of the sample of the Border Region currency and food coupon presented to Soong Ching Ling by the Administrative Committee of the Shanxi-Chaha'er-Hebei Border Region in 1944

● 1944 年 12 月 28 日，晋察冀边区行政委员会将边区票样册赠送宋庆龄，感谢她对晋察冀边区的援助。票样册内装有 1938 年至 1944 年间晋察冀边区银行发行的边区纸币和粮票票样 41 张。

1944 年国民政府颁发给宋庆龄的一等卿云勋章

The First Order Qing Yun Medal conferred to Soong Ching Ling by the Nationalist Government in 1944

● 1944 年 1 月 1 日，国民政府举行元旦纪念会，并举行了隆重的授勋仪式。宋庆龄因抗战中所做贡献获颁此章。卿云勋章于 1941 年 2 月开始颁行，分一至九等。颁授对象是对政务有勋劳之公务员及对社会贡献卓著之非公务员或外籍人士，是国民政府在抗战期间颁授的重要勋章之一。1944 年元旦获颁一等卿云勋章的除宋庆龄外，还有孔祥熙、孙科、居正、戴季陶、于右任、王宠惠、何应钦、宋美龄，共 9 人。

1945 年 10 月国民政府颁发给宋庆龄的抗战胜利勋章

Victory Medal conferred to Soong Ching Ling by the Nationalist Government in October 1945

● 1945 年 10 月 10 日，国民政府颁发政令，给抗战有功的文武官员和社会领袖人士颁发胜利勋章。宋庆龄的勋章编号为 589。勋章中间的头像是当时的国民政府主席蒋介石，勋章背面为当时中国版图轮廓图，上铸“八年抗战胜利纪念”八字。1945 年至 1946 年，抗战胜利勋章共计颁发 1 万余枚。

（1945 年）保卫中国同盟的名称改为中国福利基金会。同时也宣布了这一组织的远景，它将扩大与发展，它将致力于遭受战争创伤的恢复与建设工作。

——1950 年宋庆龄文稿《中国福利基金会工作报告》

The China Defence League was renamed into China Welfare Fund（in 1945）. The organization was trusted with the mission to expand and develop the liberated areas and commit itself to the post-war reconstruction.

—— *The Work Report of China Welfare Fund* by Soong Ching Ling in 1950

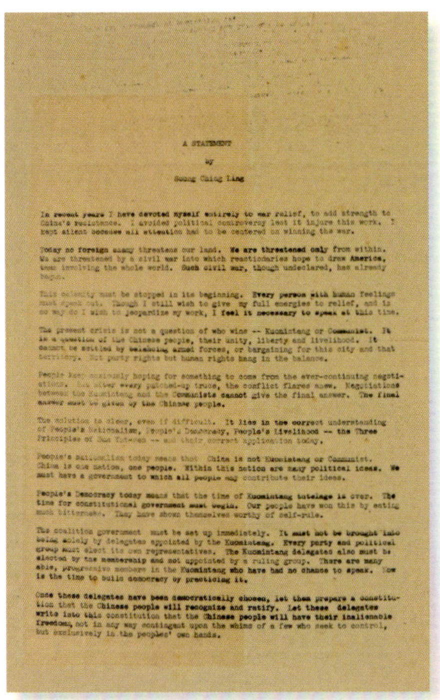

A STATEMENT

by

Soong Ching Ling

In recent years I have devoted myself entirely to war relief, to add strength to China's resistance. I avoided political controversy lest it injure this work. I kept silent because all attention had to be centered on winning the war.

Today no foreign enemy threatens our land. We are threatened only from within. We are threatened by a civil war into which reactionaries hope to draw America, thus involving the whole world. Such civil war, though undeclared, has already begun.

This calamity must be stopped in its beginning. Every person with human feelings must speak out. Though I still wish to give my full energies to relief, and in no way do I wish to jeopardize my work, I feel it necessary to speak at this time.

The present crisis is not a question of who wins -- Kuomintang or Communist. It is a question of the Chinese people, their unity, liberty and livelihood. It cannot be settled by balancing armed forces, or bargaining for this city and that territory. Not party rights but human rights hang in the balance.

People have anxiously hoping for something to come from the ever-continuing negotiations. But after every patched-up truce, the conflict flares anew. Negotiations between the Kuomintang and the Communists cannot give the final answer. The final answer must be given by the Chinese people.

The solution is clear, even if difficult. It lies in the correct understanding of People's Nationalism, People's Democracy, People's Livelihood -- the Three Principles of Sun Yat-sen -- and their correct application today.

People's Nationalism today means that China is not Kuomintang or Communist. China is one nation, one people. Within this nation are many political ideas. We must have a government to which all people may contribute their ideas.

People's Democracy today means that the time of Kuomintang tutelage is over. The time for constitutional government must begin. Our people have won this by eating much bitterness. They have shown themselves worthy of self-rule.

The coalition government must be set up immediately. It must not be brought into being solely by delegates appointed by the Kuomintang. Every party and political group must elect its own representatives. The Kuomintang delegates also must be elected by the membership and not appointed by a ruling group. There are many able, progressive members in the Kuomintang who have had no chance to speak. Now is the time to build democracy by practicing it.

Once these delegates have been democratically chosen, let them prepare a constitution that the Chinese people will recognize and ratify. Let these delegates write into this constitution that the Chinese people will have their inalienable freedoms, not in any way contingent upon the whims of a few who seek to control, but exclusively in the peoples' own hands.

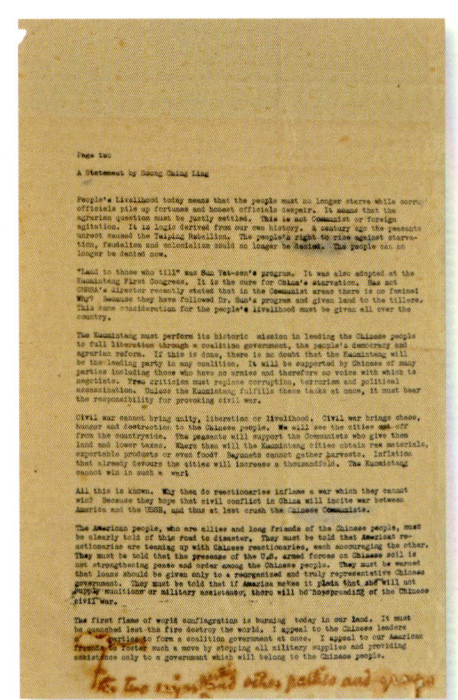

Page two

A Statement by Soong Ching Ling

People's Livelihood today means that the people must no longer starve while corrupt officials pile up fortunes and honest officials despair. It means that the agrarian question must be justly settled. This is not Communist or foreign agitation. It is logic derived from our own history. A century ago the peasants unrest caused the Taiping Rebellion. The people's right to rise against starvation, feudalism and colonialism could no longer be denied. The people can no longer be denied now.

"Land to those who till" was Sun Yat-sen's program. It was also adopted at the Kuomintang First Congress. It is the cure for China's starvation. Has not CNRRA's director recently stated that in the Communist areas there is no famine? Why? Because they have followed Dr. Sun's program and given land to the tillers. This same consideration for the people's livelihood must be given all over the country.

The Kuomintang must perform its historic mission in leading the Chinese people to full liberation through a coalition government, the people's democracy and agrarian reform. If this is done, there is no doubt that the Kuomintang will be the leading party in any coalition. It will be supported by Chinese of many parties including those who have no armies and therefore no voice with which to negotiate. Free criticism must replace corruption, terrorism and political assassination. Unless the Kuomintang fulfills these tasks at once, it must bear the responsibility for provoking civil war.

Civil war cannot bring unity, liberation or livelihood. Civil war brings chaos, hunger and destruction to the Chinese people. We will see the cities cut off from the countryside. The peasants will support the Communists who give them land and lower taxes. Where then will the Kuomintang cities obtain raw materials, exportable products or even food? Bayonets cannot gather harvests. Inflation that already devours the cities will increase a thousandfold. The Kuomintang cannot win in such a war!

All this is known. Why then do reactionaries inflame a war which they cannot win? Because they hope that civil conflict in China will incite war between America and the USSR, and thus at last crush the Chinese Communists.

The American people, who are allies and long friends of the Chinese people, must be clearly told of this road to disaster. They must be told that American reactionaries are teaming up with Chinese reactionaries, each encouraging the other. They must be told that the presence of the U.S. armed forces on Chinese soil is not strengthening peace and order among the Chinese people. They must be warned that loans should be given only to a reorganized and truly representative Chinese government. They must be told that if America makes it plain that she will not supply munitions or military assistance, there will be no spreading of the Chinese civil war.

The first flame of world conflagration is burning today in our land. It must be quenched lest the fire destroy the world. I appeal to the Chinese leaders of [illegible] parties to form a coalition government at once. I appeal to our American friends to foster such a move by stopping all military supplies and providing assistance only to a government which will belong to the Chinese people.

1946 年 7 月 22 日宋庆龄文稿《关于促成组织联合政府并呼吁美国人民制止他们的政府在军事上援助国民党的声明》

Statement Urging Coalition Government and appealing to the American People to Stop Their Government from Militarily Aiding the Kuomintang issued by Soong Ching Ling on July 22, 1946

● 1946 年 6 月，全面内战爆发。7 月 22 日，宋庆龄打破沉默在上海发表《关于促成组织联合政府并呼吁美国人民制止他们的政府在军事上援助国民党的声明》，强烈谴责国民党反动派发动反共、反人民的全面内战，呼吁美国政府停止援助国民党，国共两党组织联合政府。

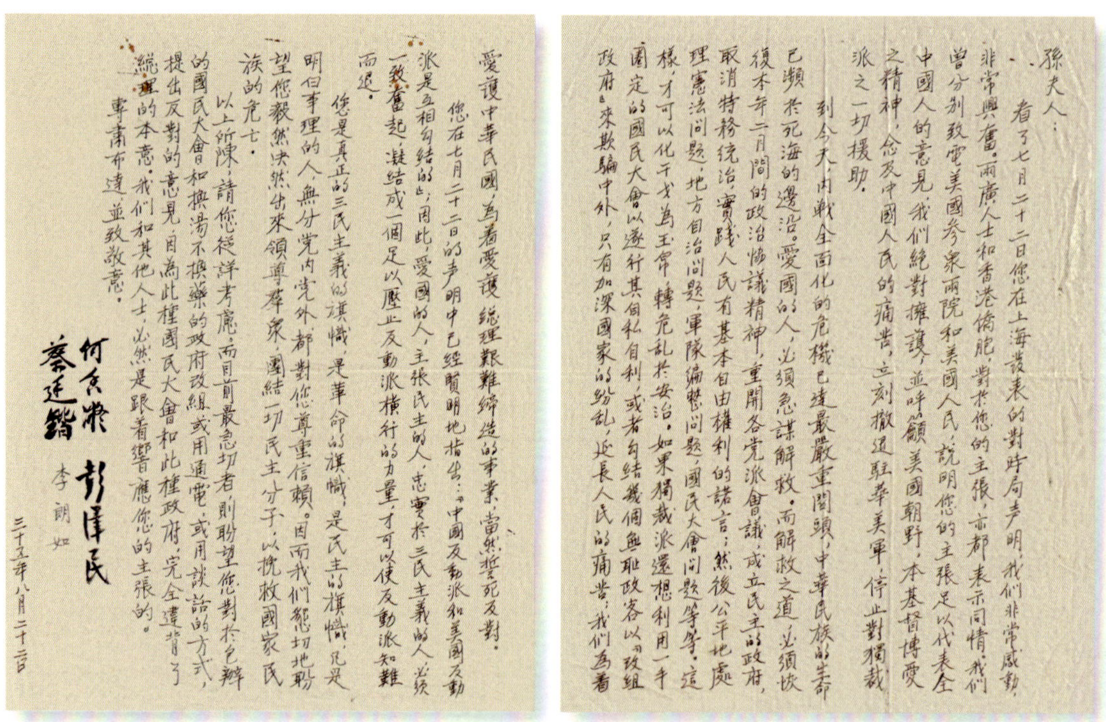

孫夫人：

看了七月二十二日您在上海發表的對時局声明，我們非常感動，非常興奮。兩廣人士和香港僑胞，對於您的主張，亦都表示同情。我們曾分別致電美國參衆兩院和美國人民，說明您的主張足以代表全中國人的意見，我們絕對擁護，並呼籲美國朝野，本基督博愛之精神，念及中國人民的痛苦，立刻撤退駐華美軍，停止對獨裁派之一切援助。

到今天，內戰全面化的危機已達最嚴重關頭，中華民族的生命已瀕於死海的邊沿。愛國的人，必須急謀解救。而解救之道，必須恢復本年二月間的政治協議精神，重開各党派會議，成立民主的政府，取消特務統治，實踐人民有基本自由權利的諾言；然後公平地處理憲法問題，地方自治問題，軍隊編整問題，國民大會問題等等。這樣，才可以化干戈為玉帛，轉危乱於安治。如果獨裁派還想利用一手圈定的國民大會以遂行其自私自利，或者勾結幾個無恥政客以"改組政府"來欺騙中外，只有加深國家的紛乱，延長人民的痛苦。我們為着愛護中華民國，為着愛護總理艱難締造的事業，當然誓死反對。

您在七月二十二日的声明中已經鮮明地指出："中國反動派和美國反動派是互相勾結的"，因此，愛國的人，主張民主的人，忠實於三民主義的人，必須一致奮起，凝結成一個足以壓止反動派橫行的力量，才可以使反動派知難而退。

您是真正的三民主義的旗幟，是革命的旗幟，是民主的旗幟，凡是明白事理的人，無分党內党外，都對您尊重信賴。因而我們懇切地盼望您毅然決然出來領導群衆，團結一切民主分子，以挽救國家民族的危亡。

以上所陳，請您從詳考慮。而目前最急切者，則盼望您對於包辦的國民大會和換湯不換藥的政府改組，或用通電，或用談話的方式，提出反對的意見。因為此種國民大會和此種政府，完全違背了總理的本意。我們和其他人士，必然是跟着響應您的主張的。

專肅布達，並致敬意。

何香凝 蔡廷鍇 彭澤民 李朗如

三十五年八月二十二日

1946 年 8 月 22 日何香凝、蔡廷锴、彭泽民、李朗如联名致宋庆龄信

A joint letter to Soong Ching Ling from He Xiangning, Cai Tingkai, Peng Zemin and Li Langru on August 22, 1946

● 1946 年 7 月 22 日宋庆龄发表的《关于促成组织联合政府并呼吁美国人民制止他们的政府在军事上援助国民党的声明》，在国内外引起广泛而强烈的反响，各界纷纷响应。8 月 22 日，在香港的民主人士何香凝、蔡廷锴、彭泽民、李朗如四人联名致函宋庆龄，称："您的主张足以代表全中国人的意见，我们绝对拥护"，希望宋庆龄"毅然决然出来领导群众"。

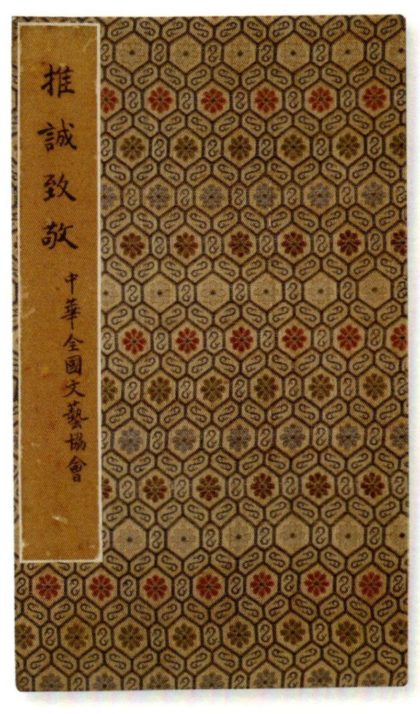

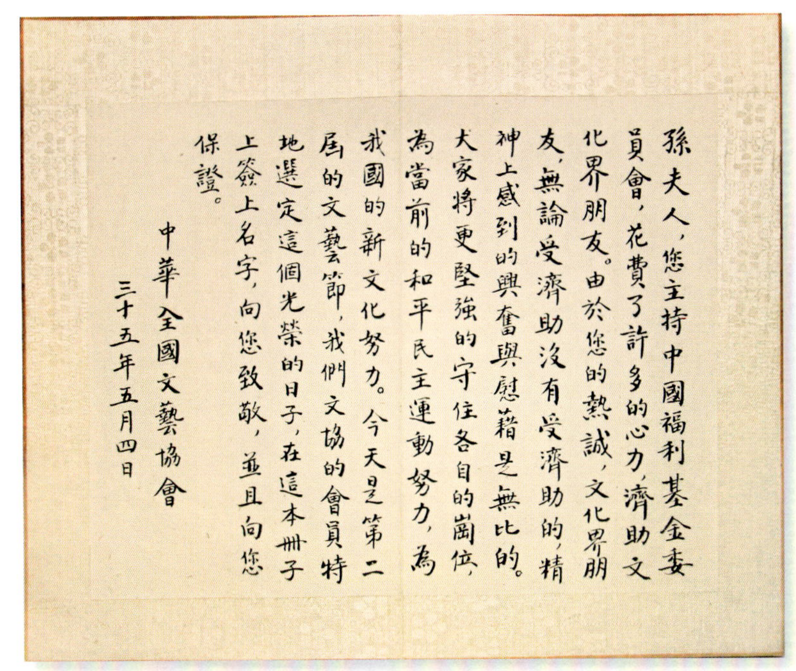

孫夫人，您主持中國福利基金委員會，花費了許多的心力，濟助文化界朋友。由於您的熱誠，文化界朋友，無論受濟助沒有受濟助的，精神上感到的興奮與慰藉是無比的。大家將更堅強的守住各自的崗位，為當前的和平民主運動努力，為我國的新文化努力。今天是第二屆的文藝節，我們文協的會員特地選定這個光榮的日子，在這本冊子上簽上名字，向您致敬，並且向您保證。

中華全國文藝協會
三十五年五月四日

1946 年 5 月中华全国文艺协会赠送宋庆龄的“推诚致敬”签名纪念册

The signature commemorative album presented to Soong Ching Ling by the China National Resistance Association of Literary and Art Workers in May 1946

● 1946 年 5 月，中华全国文艺协会在上海辣斐大戏院（今长城电影院）举办五四纪念会和文艺欣赏会。会上特向宋庆龄赠送题名为“推诚致敬”的纪念册一本，以感谢她领导的中国福利基金会在上海对文化界进步人士开展的救助活动。在纪念册上签名的有叶圣陶、赵景深、柯灵、钱锺书、杨绛、许广平、顾颉刚、陈烟桥、赵家璧、郑振铎、夏衍等文化界进步人士 82 人。

青年木刻家杨可扬、李桦赠送宋庆龄的版画

The woodcut prints presented to Soong Ching Ling by young woodcutters Yang Keyang and Li Hua

●此两件为国民党统治区青年木刻家杨可扬、李桦分别赠送宋庆龄的版画，感谢宋庆龄领导的中国福利基金会对新兴木刻版画的支持。版画刻画了战争中流离失所的难民，真实再现了当时的社会状况。杨可扬的版画作于 1947 年，并于当年 4 月 25 日赠送宋庆龄。

中国解放区救济总会驻上海办事处业务主任林仲赠送宋庆龄的《延安木刻集》
The Yan'an Woodcut Collection presented to Soong Ching Ling by Lin Zhong, director of the Shanghai Office of Chinese Liberated Area Relief Administration

● 1946 年中国解放区救济总会在上海设立办事处，与宋庆龄领导的中国福利基金会合作，争取从联合国善后救济总署和其他官方团体所提供的国际救济资金和物资中，为解放区争取份额，缓解困难。1946 年 9 月 18 日，中华全国木刻协会在上海举办“抗战八年木刻展览会”，延安的木刻作品也在展览会中展出，得到宋庆龄等人的热情赞助。9 月 3 日展览开幕前，中国解放区救济总会驻上海办事处业务主任林仲向宋庆龄赠送了这本《延安木刻集》，感谢她为解放区争取的援助。这本木刻集汇集了 70 余幅木刻作品，作品用宣纸拓印，再在马兰草纸上裱衬后装订成册，表现的内容为解放区军民现实生活和抗战斗争。

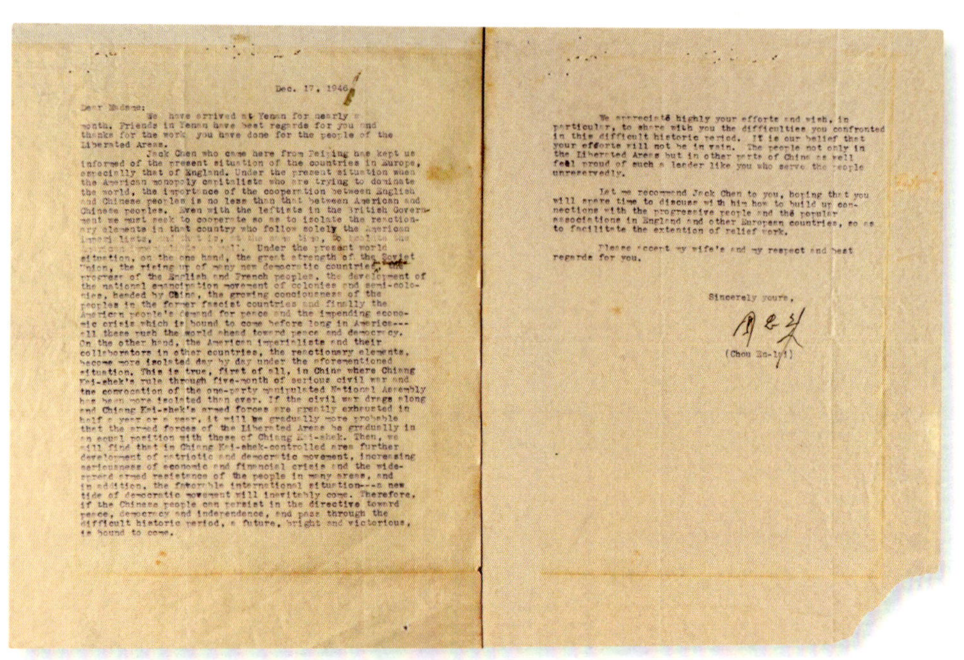

Dec. 17, 1946

Dear Madame:

We have arrived at Yenan for nearly a month. Friends in Yenan have best regards for you and thanks for the work you have done for the people of the Liberated Areas.

Jack Chen who came here from Peiping has kept us informed of the present situation of the countries in Europe, especially that of England. Under the present situation when the American monopoly capitalists who are trying to dominate the world, the importance of the cooperation between English and Chinese peoples is no less than that between American and Chinese peoples. Even with the leftists in the British Government we must seek to cooperate so as to isolate the reactionary elements in that country who follow solely the American imperialists, [illegible]. Under the present world situation, on the one hand, the great strength of the Soviet Union, the rising up of many new democratic countries, the progress of the English and French peoples, the development of the national emancipation movement of colonies and semi-colonies, headed by China, the growing conciousness of the peoples in the former fascist countries and finally the American people's demand for peace and the impending economic crisis which is bound to come before long in America---all these push the world ahead toward peace and democracy. On the other hand, the American imperialists and their collaborators in other countries, the reactionary elements, become more isolated day by day under the aforementioned situation. This is true, first of all, in China where Chiang Kai-shek's rule through five-month of serious civil war and the convocation of the one-party manipulated National Assembly has been more isolated than ever. If the civil war drags along and Chiang Kai-shek's armed forces are greatly exhausted in half a year or a year, it will be gradually more probable that the armed forces of the Liberated Areas be gradually in an equal position with those of Chiang Kai-shek. Then, we will find that in Chiang Kai-shek-controlled area further development of patriotic and democratic movement, increasing seriousness of economic and financial crisis and the wide-spread armed resistance of the people in many areas, and in addition, the favorable international situation---a new tide of democratic movement will inevitably come. Therefore, if the Chinese people can persist in the directive toward peace, democracy and independence, and pass through the difficult historic period, a future, bright and victorious, is bound to come.

We appreciate highly your efforts and wish, in particular, to share with you the difficulties you confronted in this difficult historic period. It is our belief that your efforts will not be in vain. The people not only in the Liberated Areas but in other parts of China as well feel proud of such a leader like you who serve the people unreservedly.

Let me recommend Jack Chen to you, hoping that you will spare time to discuss with him how to build up connections with the progressive people and the popular associations in England and other European countries, so as to facilitate the extention of relief work.

Please accept my wife's and my respect and best regards for you.

Sincerely yours,

周恩来

(Chou En-lai)

1946年12月17日周恩来致宋庆龄信

Zhou Enlai's letter to Soong Ching Ling on December 17, 1946

●抗日战争胜利后，宋庆龄将保卫中国同盟改组为中国福利基金会，继续支援解放区的医疗卫生事业。1946年12月17日，周恩来在延安致函宋庆龄，对她一贯支持解放区的工作表示感谢。函谓：“延安的朋友们都惦念着您，感谢您为解放区人民所做的工作。”周恩来还在信中分析了国内外形势，并对如何扩大海外援助提出了建议。

1947 年宋庆龄在中国福利基金会第一儿童福利站工地

Soong Ching Ling at the construction site of the First Children's Welfare Station of the China Welfare Fund in 1947

● 1947 年 4 月，宋庆龄将中国福利基金会在上海沪西贫民区胶州路 725 号（晋元小学内）创办的儿童图书阅览室扩充为第一儿童福利站，图为宋庆龄与中国福利基金会执行委员比尔·鲍威尔在第一儿童福利站工地。福利站建成后，宋庆龄曾亲往视察，并指导小读者看书识字。从 1947 年起，宋庆龄在上海的工人聚居区建立了三个儿童福利站，为邻近的孩子们提供文化识字、医疗营养等方面的救助。

儿童剧作家董林肯赠送宋庆龄的苏联儿童剧本《表》

Watch, a Soviet children's drama presented to Soong Ching Ling by Dong Linken, a children playwright

● 1947 年 4 月 10 日，宋庆龄创办的儿童剧团在上海兰心大戏院上演鲁迅翻译、董林肯改编的苏联儿童剧《表》。宋庆龄专门为首演题词：“《表》是一出深刻而动人的儿童剧，……它不仅对儿童有很大的教育作用，同时也给予从事儿童教育者一个明确的启示。”此件为儿童剧作家董林肯赠送宋庆龄的儿童剧本《表》，由立化出版社 1947 年出版，扉页写有“庆龄先生指正 晚 十月十六日”。这出儿童剧描写了十月革命胜利后，布尔什维克党拯救、教育流浪儿童的故事。首演时，许多小观众都是宋庆龄请来的儿童福利站的孩子，宋庆龄与他们一同观看了这场儿童剧。

宋庆龄保存的“三毛乐园会”纪念徽章

The commemorative medal of *Sanmao Paradise* preserved by Soong Ching Ling

● 1949 年春，随着上海街头的流浪儿童愈益增多，宋庆龄举办“三毛乐园会”和“三毛生活展览会”为流浪儿童募资义卖，活动所得全部交予中国福利基金会下三个儿童福利站、儿童剧团和育才学校作经费使用。漫画家张乐平特地为“三毛乐园会”设计了一枚别致的纪念徽章，宋庆龄珍藏了其中一枚。

《孙夫人的报告——中国福利基金会的工作》

Madame Sun Reports-The Story of the China Welfare Fund

● 1947 年 6 月，中国福利基金会发布一份工作报告，这份报告 1948 年由美国兰登书屋编印为《孙夫人的报告》出版发行。在这本精美的宣传册中，宋庆龄以其个人名义向海外援华团体及国际友人用英文全面介绍中国福利基金会及其工作情况，并希望通过推销该报告来扩大宣传，募集物资。《孙夫人的报告》封面为宋庆龄 1944 年在重庆所摄照片，腰封为原中国战区参谋长约瑟夫·沃伦·史迪威的夫人温妮费德·史迪威写给此书的献词。报告刊载了宋庆龄写给海外朋友的一封信，并详细介绍了中国福利基金会所援助的解放区医疗卫生、儿童保育机构的情况及存在的困难等，还刊登了中国福利基金会与海内外相关机构开展合作的情况及今后的工作展望等信息。

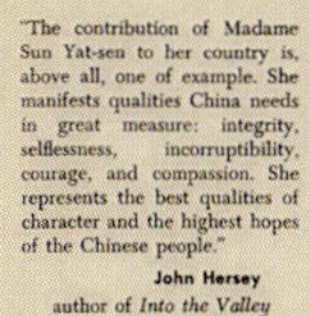

"The contribution of Madame Sun Yat-sen to her country is, above all, one of example. She manifests qualities China needs in great measure: integrity, selflessness, incorruptibility, courage, and compassion. She represents the best qualities of character and the highest hopes of the Chinese people."

John Hersey

author of *Into the Valley* and *A Bell for Adano*

A Personal Letter from Madame Sun Yat-sen

DEAR FRIENDS:

This is the fourth report we are making from China, bringing you up-to-date on the activities of the China Welfare Fund.

The last time such a book was published, in 1943, we were known as the China Defence League. Since that time the Anti-Japanese War has ended and we have had to broaden our perspective, aim at new objectives and take on many strenuous activities to meet heartbreaking demands for help. Your generous aid in the past has not only kept us going, but has inspired us to cultivate resources in China itself. For this, please accept our deepfelt thanks. Now we wish to appeal for your continued support of the Chinese people's struggle.

The new emphasis of our program is to give the people a chance to live and build. For many of them this is the first opportunity they have ever had. Providing this chance to live and build is the logical basis for a welfare program. China's needs are cen-

5

tered about rehabilitation, reconstruction and forging for the future. However, it is a job which must be accomplished in the face of mounting difficulties.

This is a crucial period for China, and in fact, for the whole world. All of us are on the threshold of being able to live like human beings with one another. This much-sought condition is certainly the demand of common men and women all over the earth. Yet, there are those who would slam the door in our faces, cutting off decency, democracy and livelihood. They would substitute or support the very things against which the allies have but so recently finished fighting—fascist tactics, political and economic slavery. This group must be shown that the rank and file of all nations will not be denied in their quest for peace and unity.

One way to make clear that you want the people to win is by joining their efforts. Your interest in their fight must be continued. Your contributions must be maintained for those projects which have their starting point in the cause of the people and whose effects actually reach down to them.

To assure our supporters and ourselves that the China Welfare Fund has always operated at this proper level, we have for years been the exponent of "Help the People to Help Themselves." With the exception of a few emergency activities, we believe in getting to the base of things. In relief terms this means originating and sustaining projects which work to support themselves. This is our guiding principle.

The China Welfare Fund has one other yardstick by which it functions: "Aid Without Discrimination." There is no section of China which does not need outside support. The years of conflict have taken their toll. Therefore, we act upon the precept that where help is needed, where the people are helping themselves, that is where the help will be sent. No part of the land is excluded, and we object to and fight against obstruction of relief and rehabilitation for political reasons. Our projects extend to people in every corner of China no matter how they reason or where they reside. Of this record we are proud.

Friends, your continued backing for such a program and principles is sought because it is still sorely needed. We require your aid once again so that the Chinese people can freely dedicate

6

their lives to make themselves responsible citizens of this modern world. It is an obligation all of us have. Help us in our task, and you help yourselves.

With greetings,

Very sincerely yours,

"The wisest person I met in the Orient was Madame Soong Ching Ling, the gentle, soft-spoken widow of Dr. Sun Yat-sen, China's first President. Last July in her appeal to the American people to withdraw their armed forces from China Madame Sun said: 'Every person with human feeling must speak out. The present crisis is not a question of who wins, the Kuomintang or the Communists. It is a question of the Chinese people, their unity, and livelihood. It cannot be settled by balancing armies or bargaining for this city and that territory. Not party rights, but human rights, hang in the balance.'

"Millions of Chinese who are not Kuomintang, not Communist, realize as Madame Sun does, that only by the mightiest collective effort of all its people will China ever rise from its bed of anguish."

Richard E. Lauterbach

in his book "Danger from the East"

7

宋庆龄致海外朋友的信

A letter to overseas friends from Soong Ching Ling

我可以告诉你，这里正在发生的一切令人振奋。孙中山先生的所有理想正在被有力地付诸实施。这些理想和其他一些重大的计划一起，使这里成为一个真正的崭新的中国。我们已确立了自己应有的地位，同世界上其他的伟大民族一同前进。

——1951 年宋庆龄致克劳特夫人信

I can tell you that what is taking place here is truly inspiring. All of the dreams that Dr. Sun had are being forcefully implemented. All of these plus other important plans are making this truly a new China. We have taken our rightful place along the other great nations of the world.

——Soong Ching Ling to Mrs. Crouter in 1951

20 世纪 50 年代宋庆龄在北京方巾巷寓所留影

Soong Ching Ling in her residence at Fangjin Lane in Beijing in the 1950s

1949 年宋庆龄手稿《向中国共产党致敬》

Manuscript of Soong Ching Ling's article *Salute to the Communist Party of China* in 1949

● 1949 年 6 月 30 日，宋庆龄受邀参加中共中央华东局、中共上海市委在上海举行的“七一”纪念会，庆祝中国共产党成立 28 周年。宋庆龄为此专门撰写祝词，但因庆祝大会当日身体不适，请邓颖超代为宣读。此件为祝词英文原稿译为中文后宋庆龄的亲笔誊写件。宋庆龄以散文诗的形式表达了她对中国共产党、中国人民解放军的崇敬之情，热烈欢呼人民的胜利已在眼前，称中国共产党为“我们的领袖”，满怀激情地“向中国共产党致敬”。7 月 2 日，《人民日报》全文发表了宋庆龄祝词。

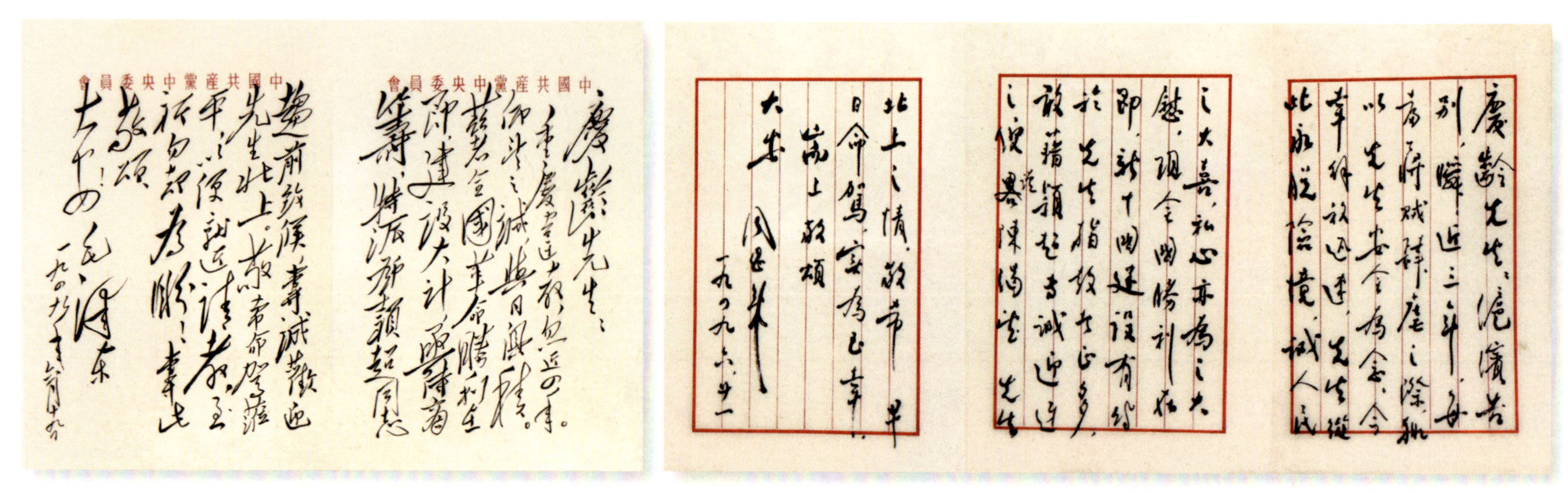

中國共產黨中央委員會

慶齡先生：

重慶違教，忽近四年。仰望之誠，與日俱積。茲者全國革命勝利在即，建設大計，亟待商籌，特派鄧穎超同志趨前致候，專誠歡迎

中國共產黨中央委員會

先生北上，敬希命駕莅平，以便就近請教，至祈勿卻為盼！專此。敬頌

大安！

毛澤東

一九四九年六月十九日

慶齡先生：滬濱告別，瞬近三年，每當蔣賊肆虐之際，輒以先生安全為念，今幸解放迅速，先生從此永脫險境，誠人民之大喜，私心亦為之大慰。現全國勝利在即，新中國建設有待於先生指教者正多，敬藉穎超專誠迎迓之便，略（謹）陳渴望先生北上之情，敬希早日命駕，實為至幸。端此敬頌

大安

周恩來

一九四九、六、廿一

1949 年 6 月 19 日毛泽东致宋庆龄信、1949 年 6 月 21 日周恩来致宋庆龄信

A letter from Mao Zedong to Soong Ching Ling on June 19, 1949; a letter from Zhou Enlai to Soong Ching Ling on June 21, 1949

● 1949 年 6 月 15 日至 19 日，中国人民政治协商会议筹备会第一次全体会议在北平中南海举行。毛泽东于 19 日在香山双清别墅写信给宋庆龄，邀请宋庆龄赴北平共商建国大计。21 日，周恩来亦致信宋庆龄请其北上，毛泽东专门将周恩来信中的“略陈”改为“谨陈”，体现出中共中央对宋庆龄的尊敬。25 日，邓颖超受中共中央委托携带毛泽东、周恩来的亲笔信专程抵达上海，邀请宋庆龄北上。30 日，宋庆龄同意到北平参加中国人民政治协商会议。8 月 26 日，宋庆龄在邓颖超、廖梦醒等陪同下乘火车离开上海，于 28 日抵达北平，毛泽东、朱德、刘少奇、周恩来等中共中央领导人亲自到火车站迎接。当晚，毛泽东设宴为宋庆龄洗尘，热烈欢迎她来北平共商国家大事。此两封信 1981 年 11 月从上海宋庆龄故居清理出来后由中央档案馆收藏。

1949 年 9 月 21 日宋庆龄在中国人民政治协商会议第一届全体会议上讲话

Soong Ching Ling addressing the First Plenary Session of the CPPCC on September 21, 1949

● 1949 年 9 月 21 日至 30 日，宋庆龄作为特别邀请代表出席中国人民政治协商会议第一届全体会议，并当选为中央人民政府副主席，成为中华人民共和国的缔造者之一。图为 9 月 21 日宋庆龄在大会上发表讲话。

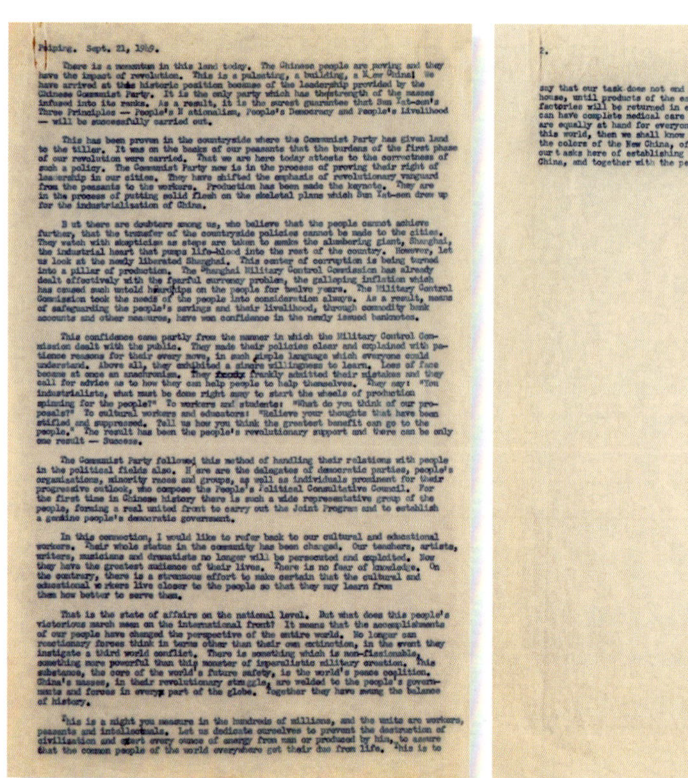

Peiping. Sept. 21, 1949.

There is a momentum in this land today. The Chinese people are moving and they have the impact of revolution. This is a pulsating, a building, a New China! We have arrived at this historic position because of the leadership provided by the Chinese Communist Party. It is the only party which has the strength of the masses infused into its ranks. As a result, it is the surest guarantee that Sun Yat-sen's Three Principles — People's Nationalism, People's Democracy and People's Livelihood — will be successfully carried out.

This has been proven in the countryside where the Communist Party has given land to the tiller. It was on the backs of our peasants that the burdens of the first phase of our revolution were carried. That we are here today attests to the correctness of such a policy. The Communist Party now is in the process of proving their right of leadership in our cities. They have shifted the emphasis of revolutionary vanguard from the peasants to the workers. Production has been made the keynote. They are in the process of putting solid flesh on the skeletal plans which Sun Yat-sen drew up for the industrialization of China.

But there are doubters among us, who believe that the people cannot achieve further, that the transfer of the countryside policies cannot be made to the cities. They watch with skepticism as steps are taken to awake the slumbering giant, Shanghai, the industrial heart that pumps life-blood into the rest of the country. However, let us look at the newly liberated Shanghai. This center of corruption is being turned into a pillar of production. The Shanghai Military Control Commission has already dealt effectively with the fearful currency problem, the galloping inflation which has caused such untold hardships on the people for twelve years. The Military Control Commission took the needs of the people into consideration always. As a result, means of safeguarding the people's savings and their livelihood, through commodity bank accounts and other measures, have won confidence in the newly issued banknotes.

This confidence came partly from the manner in which the Military Control Commission dealt with the public. They made their policies clear and explained with patience reasons for their every move, in such simple language which everyone could understand. Above all, they exhibited a sincere willingness to learn. Loss of face became at once an anachronism. They frankly admitted their mistakes and they call for advice as to how they can help people to help themselves. They say: "You industrialists, what must be done right away to start the wheels of production spinning for the people?" To workers and students: "What do you think of our proposals?" To cultural workers and educators: "Relieve your thoughts that have been stifled and suppressed. Tell us how you think the greatest benefit can go to the people." The result has been the people's revolutionary support and there can be only one result — Success.

The Communist Party followed this method of handling their relations with people in the political fields also. Here are the delegates of democratic parties, people's organizations, minority races and groups, as well as individuals prominent for their progressive outlook, who compose the People's Political Consultative Council. For the first time in Chinese history there is such a wide representative group of the people, forming a real united front to carry out the Joint Program and to establish a genuine people's democratic government.

In this connection, I would like to refer back to our cultural and educational workers. Their whole status in the community has been changed. Our teachers, artists, writers, musicians and dramatists no longer will be persecuted and exploited. Now they have the greatest audience of their lives. There is no fear of knowledge. On the contrary, there is a strenuous effort to make certain that the cultural and educational workers live closer to the people so that they may learn from them how better to serve them.

That is the state of affairs on the national level. But what does this people's victorious march mean on the international front? It means that the accomplishments of our people have changed the perspective of the entire world. No longer can reactionary forces think in terms other than their own extinction, in the event they instigate a third world conflict. There is something which is non-fissionable, something more powerful than this monster of imperialistic military creation. This substance, the core of the world's future safety, is the world's peace coalition. China's masses, in their revolutionary struggle, are welded to the people's governments and forces in every part of the globe. Together they have swung the balance of history.

This is a might you measure in the hundreds of millions, and the units are workers, peasants and intellectuals. Let us dedicate ourselves to prevent the destruction of civilization and exert every ounce of energy from man or produced by him, to assure that the common people of the world everywhere get their due from life. This is to

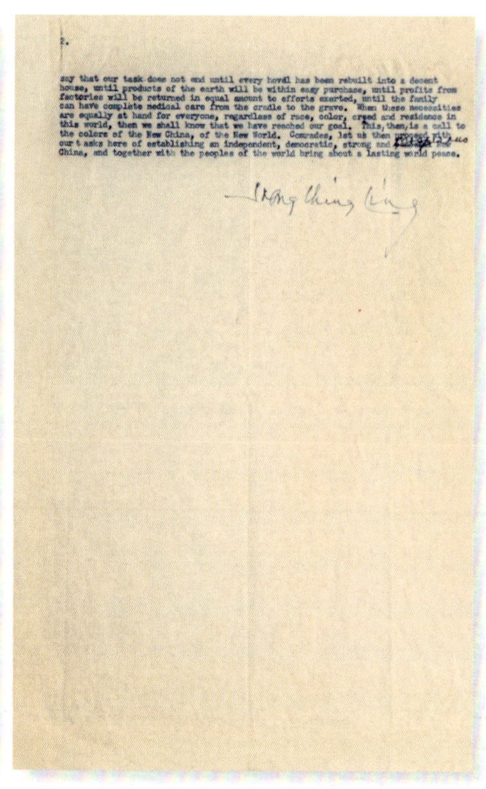

2.

say that our task does not end until every hovel has been rebuilt into a decent house, until products of the earth will be within easy purchase, until profits from factories will be returned in equal amount to efforts exerted, until the family can have complete medical care from the cradle to the grave. When these necessities are equally at hand for everyone, regardless of race, color, creed and residence in this world, then we shall know that we have reached our goal. This, then, is a call to the colors of the New China, of the New World. Comrades, let us then proceed with our tasks here of establishing an independent, democratic, strong and prosperous New China, and together with the peoples of the world bring about a lasting world peace.

Soong Ching Ling

1949 年 9 月 21 日宋庆龄在中国人民政治协商会议第一届全体会议上的讲话英文原稿

Soong Ching Ling' s original speech in English at the First Plenary Session of the CPPCC delivered on September 21,1949

● 1949 年 9 月 21 日，中国人民政治协商会议第一届全体会议在中南海怀仁堂隆重开幕。宋庆龄作为特别邀请代表在会上发表讲话。此件为讲话英文原稿。宋庆龄在讲话中号召大家建设一个独立、民主、和平与富强的新中国，还指出：“我们达到今天的历史地位，是由于中国共产党的领导，这是唯一拥有人民大众力量的政党。孙中山的民族、民权、民生三大主义的胜利实现，因此得到了最可靠的保证。”

1952 年 10 月 1 日宋庆龄与毛泽东、周恩来等在北京天安门城楼上检阅群众游行队伍和人民武装力量
On October 1, 1952, Soong Ching Ling with Mao Zedong, Zhou Enlai and others reviewing the mass parades and the people's armed forces on the Tian' anmen Rostrum in Beijing

1949—1953

第一一四號

入席証

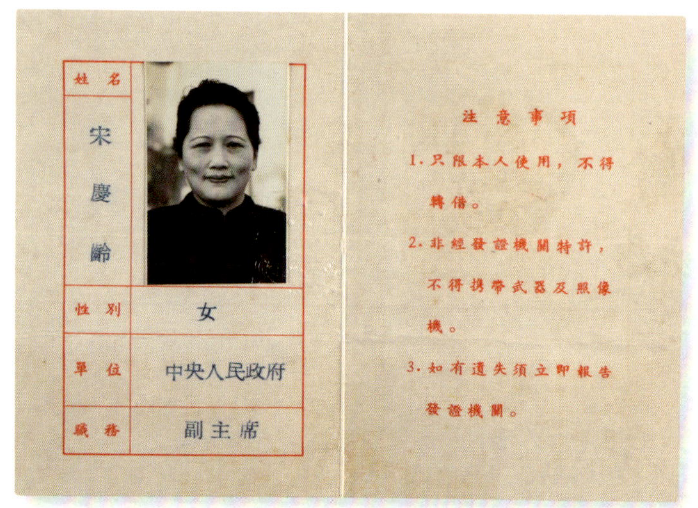

姓名	宋慶齡
性別	女
單位	中央人民政府
職務	副主席

注意事項

1. 只限本人使用，不得轉借。
2. 非經發證機關特許，不得携帶武器及照像機。
3. 如有遺失須立即報告發證機關。

1953 年宋庆龄的国庆典礼入席证

Soong Ching Ling's attendance certificate for National Day Ceremony in 1953

●宋庆龄 1953 年使用的国庆典礼入席证，编号为“第一一四号”，内页贴有宋庆龄肖像照，为 1951 年宋庆龄在北京所摄。单位和职务分别填写“中央人民政府”和“副主席”字样。

1956年10月宋庆龄与毛泽东、周恩来、陈毅、张闻天在中南海

Soong Ching Ling with Mao Zedong, Zhou Enlai, Chen Yi and Zhang Wentian in Sea Palaces in October 1956

● 1956年10月初，宋庆龄参加完中国共产党第八次全国代表大会离京返沪前，与毛泽东等在中南海留影。左起依次为张闻天、毛泽东、宋庆龄、周恩来、陈毅。

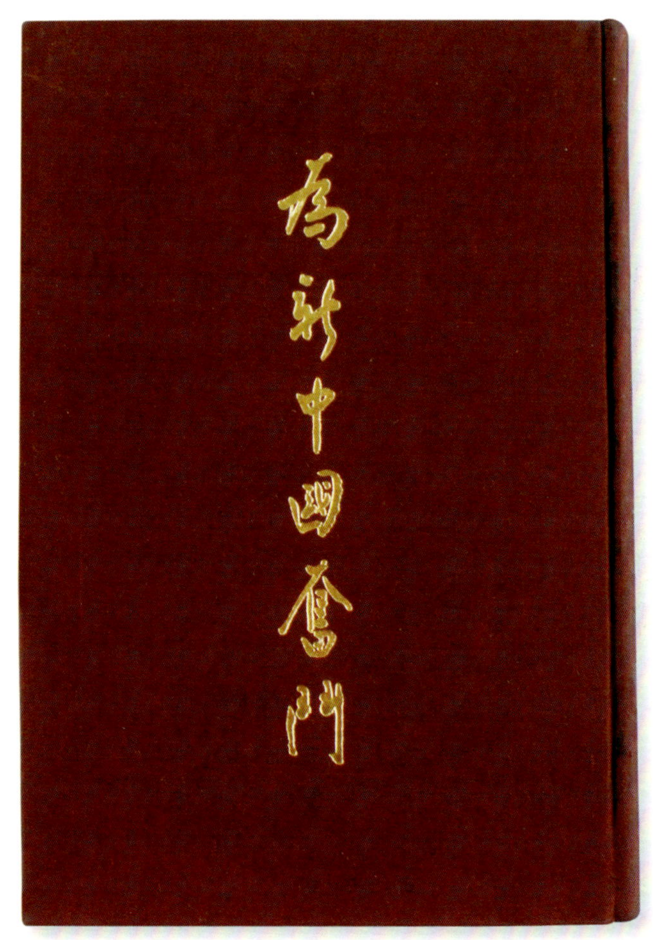

宋庆龄著作《为新中国奋斗》中文版

Soong Ching Ling's work *The Struggle for New China*（Chinese version）

●中华人民共和国建立初期，宋庆龄将自己多年来公开发表的文章结集出版，并取名为《为新中国奋斗》，由周恩来题写书名。1952 年 9 月，人民出版社和外文出版社分别出版中、英文版。文集收录了宋庆龄 1927 年 7 月至 1952 年 7 月间发表的讲演、文章、声明等共计 64 篇。

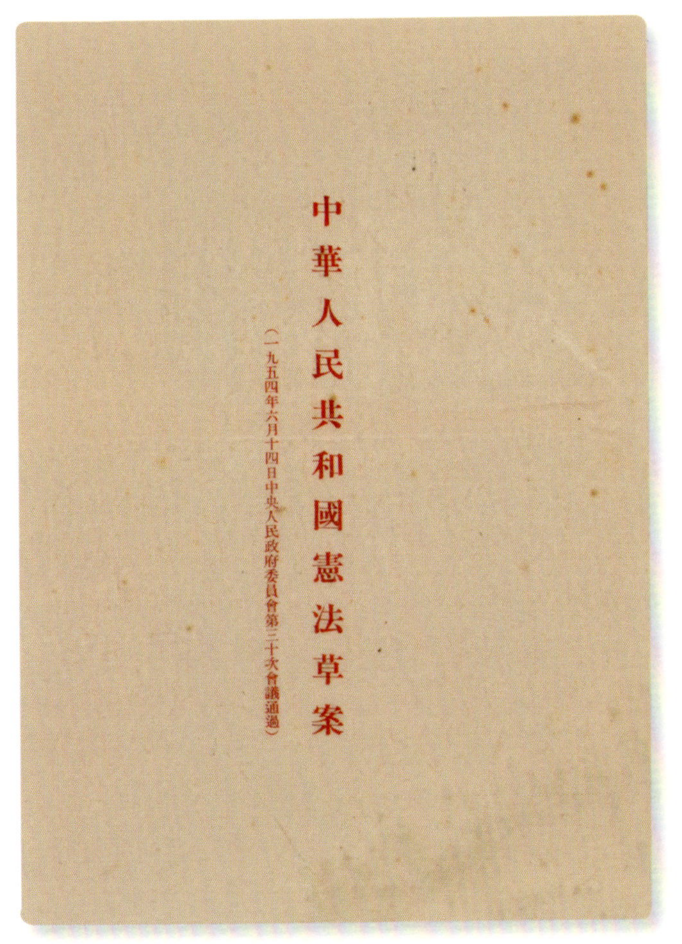

中華人民共和國憲法草案

（一九五四年六月十四日中央人民政府委員會第三十次會議通過）

1954 年宋庆龄参与讨论和审议的《中华人民共和国宪法草案》

The Draft Constitution of the People's Republic of China discussed and reviewed by Soong Ching Ling in 1954

● 1954 年 9 月，新中国第一部宪法《中华人民共和国宪法》诞生。宋庆龄作为宪法起草委员会委员，阅读研究了大量中外有关制宪的书籍和文件，积极参与制定宪法草案的工作。此件宋庆龄参与讨论和审议的《中华人民共和国宪法草案》，由 1954 年 6 月 14 日中央人民政府委员会第三十次会议通过。在这次会议上，宋庆龄发表了重要讲话，她说，宪法草案初稿的“每一字句都经过千锤百炼，每一条文都通过事实考验，我们的宪法将成为每一个公民自己的公约般的条文”。《中华人民共和国宪法草案》在全国公布交付人民群众讨论后，又再度进行了修改和补充。

宋庆龄著作《新中国向前迈进——东北旅行印象记》

Soong Ching Ling's work *New China is Marching Forward - Impressions of the Travel to Northeast China*

●《新中国向前迈进——东北旅行印象记》1951 年 7 月由人民出版社出版，记述了宋庆龄 1950 年对东北农村和土地改革、人民工厂、城市福利等的考察印象，通过大量事实与数据描述了东北城乡巨变，以此表明新中国正在向光辉的未来迈进。《新中国向前迈进——东北旅行印象记》全文发表于 1951 年 5 月 1 日的《人民日报》。

1955 年 6 月宋庆龄在松江县农村视察

Soong Ching Ling inspecting the rural area in the Songjiang Country in June 1955

● 1955 年 6 月，宋庆龄视察了全国水稻丰产模范陈永康所在的松江县（今上海市松江区）联民农业生产合作社，她在泥泞的阡陌上来回步行 10 余里，巡视了田地、水渠和副业生产，访问了陈永康等社员的家庭。

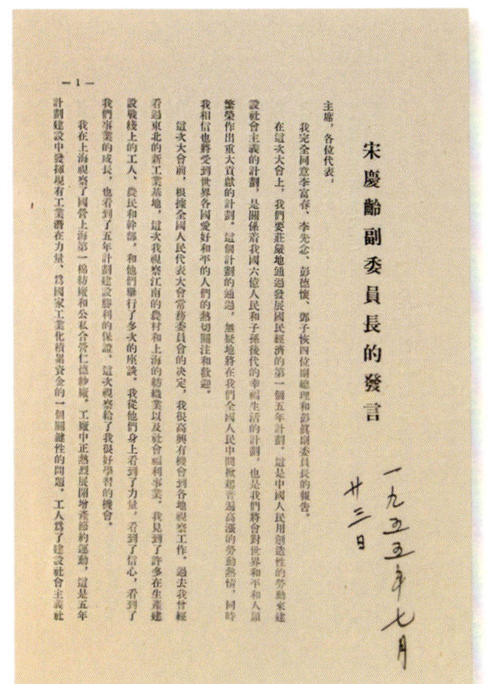

宋慶齡副委員長的發言

一九五五年七月廿三日

主席，各位代表：

我完全同意李富春、李先念、彭德懷、鄧子恢四位副總理和彭真副委員長的報告。

在這次大會上，我們要莊嚴地通過發展國民經濟的第一個五年計劃。這是中國人民用創造性的勞動來建設社會主義的計劃，是關係着我國六億人民和子孫後代的幸福生活的計劃，也是我們將會對世界和平和人類繁榮作出重大貢獻的計劃。這個計劃的通過，無疑地將在我們全國人民中間掀起普遍高漲的勞動熱情，同時我相信也將受到世界各國愛好和平的人們的熱切關注和歡迎。

這次大會前，根據全國人民代表大會常務委員會的決定，我很高興有機會到各地視察工作。過去我曾經看過東北的新工業基地，這次我視察江南的農村和上海的紡織業以及社會福利事業。我見到了許多在生產建設戰綫上的工人、農民和幹部，和他們舉行了多次的座談。我從他們身上看到了力量，看到了信心，看到了我們事業的成長，也看到了五年計劃建設勝利的保證。這次視察給了我很好學習的機會。

我在上海視察了國營上海第一棉紡廠和公私合營仁德紗廠。工廠中正熱烈展開增產節約運動，這是五年計劃建設中發揮現有工業潛在力量、爲國家工業化積累資金的一個關鍵性的問題。工人爲了建設社會主義社

— 1 —

1955 年 7 月宋庆龄出席第一届全国人民代表大会第二次会议的讲话稿

A speech of Soong Ching Ling in July 1955 at the Second Session of the First National People's Congress

● 自 1954 年起，宋庆龄先后当选为第一、第四、第五届全国人民代表大会常务委员会副委员长。她到全国各地视察，认真听取基层干部和广大群众的意见和要求，针对我国社会主义建设中遇到的问题，提出了切实可行的意见和建议。宋庆龄在这篇讲话稿中谈到视察江南农村和上海纺织业及社会福利事业的情况、感受和意见。1955 年 7 月 24 日，该文以《为了社会主义，为了和平》为题发表在《人民日报》上。

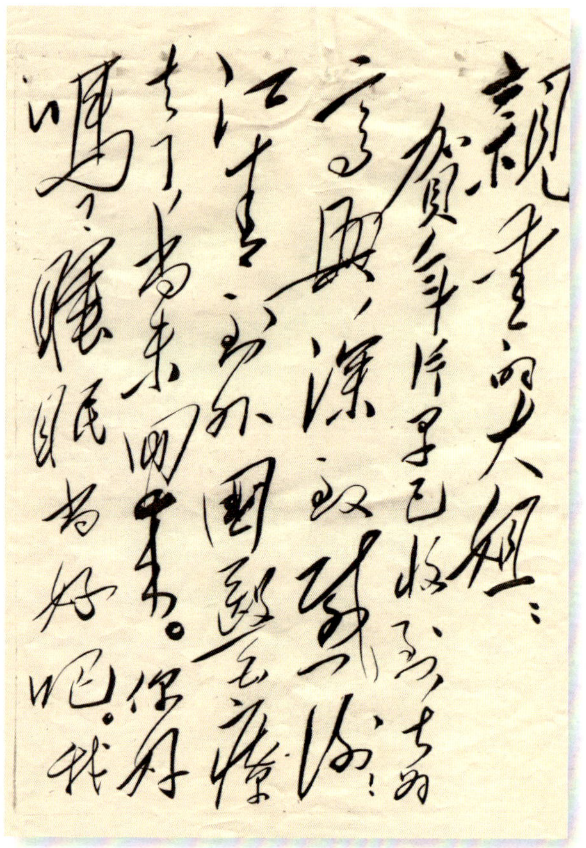

亲爱的大姐：

贺年片早已收到，甚为高兴，深致感谢！江青到外国医疗去了，尚未回来。你好吗？睡眠尚好吧。我

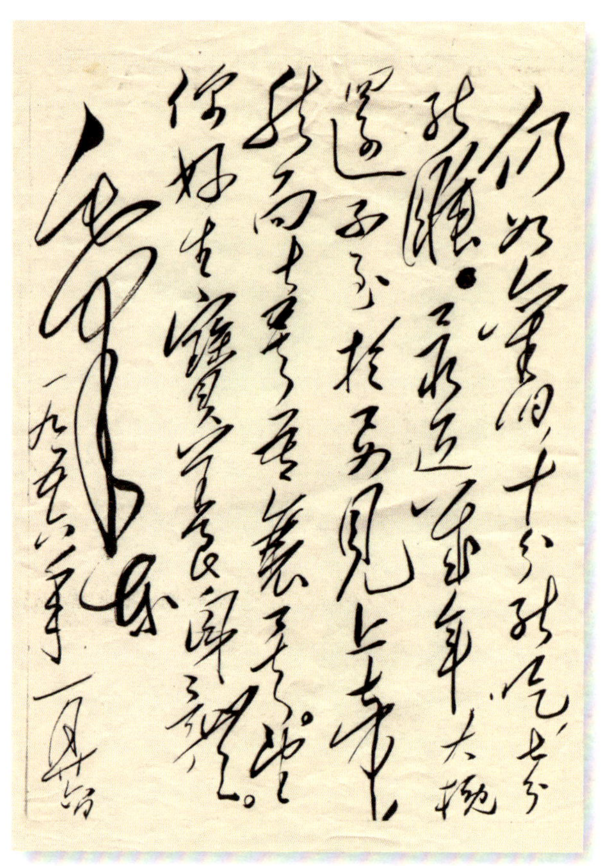

仍如旧，十分能吃，七分能睡。最近几年大概还不至于要见上帝，然而甚矣吾衰矣。望你好生宝养身体。

毛泽东

一九五六年一月廿六日

1956 年 1 月 26 日毛泽东致宋庆龄信

A letter from Mao Zedong to Soong Ching Ling on January 26, 1956

● 1956 年元旦，毛泽东收到了宋庆龄祝贺新年的卡片，即复信宋庆龄表示感谢。此件为 1956 年 1 月 26 日毛泽东复宋庆龄信，信中说：“亲爱的大姐，贺年片早已收到，甚为高兴，深致感谢！……你好吗？睡眠尚好吧。我仍如旧，十分能吃，七分能睡。最近几年大概还不至于要见上帝，然而甚矣吾衰矣。望你好生宝养身体。”此信原件 1981 年 11 月从上海宋庆龄故居清理出来后由中央档案馆收藏。

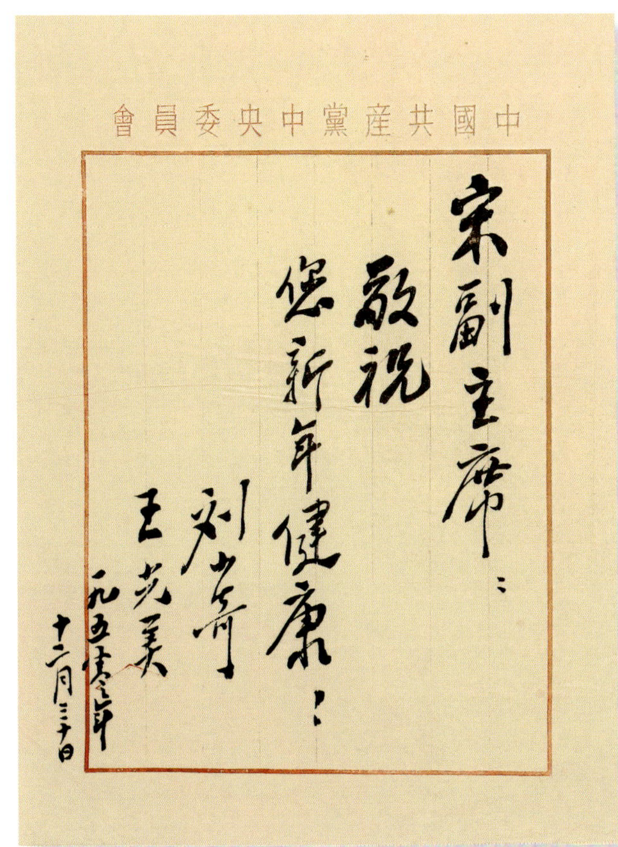
中國共產黨中央委員會

宋副主席：

敬祝

您新年健康！

刘少奇

王光美

一九五〇年十二月三十日

1950 年 12 月 30 日刘少奇、王光美致宋庆龄信

A letter from Liu Shaoqi and Wang Guangmei to Soong Ching Ling on December 30, 1950

●此件刘少奇与王光美 1950 年 12 月 30 日致宋庆龄的信，敬祝她“新年健康”。此信原件 1981 年 11 月从上海宋庆龄故居清理出来后由中央档案馆收藏。

中國福利會托兒所

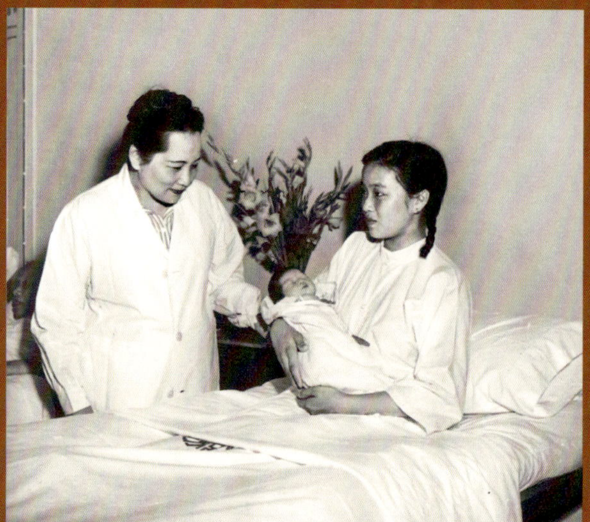

1950年，宋庆龄将中国福利基金会改名为中国福利会，致力于新中国妇女儿童福利事业。在宋庆龄的领导下，中国福利会创办了儿童剧团（剧院）、托儿所、幼儿园、《儿童时代》杂志、国际和平妇幼保健院、少年宫等妇幼保健和少儿文化教育机构等，开展了一系列实验性、示范性的工作和科学研究。

In 1950, Soong Ching Ling changed the name of the China Welfare Fund to the China Welfare Institute, dedicated to the cause of women and children welfare of new China. The China Welfare Institute led by Soong Ching Ling, established facilities and magazines such as the Children's Art Theater, Nursery, Kindergarten, *Children's Epoch*, the International Peace Maternity & Child Health Hospital, Children's Palace, carried out experimental, exemplary work and scientific research for maternal and child health care as well as children's culture and education.

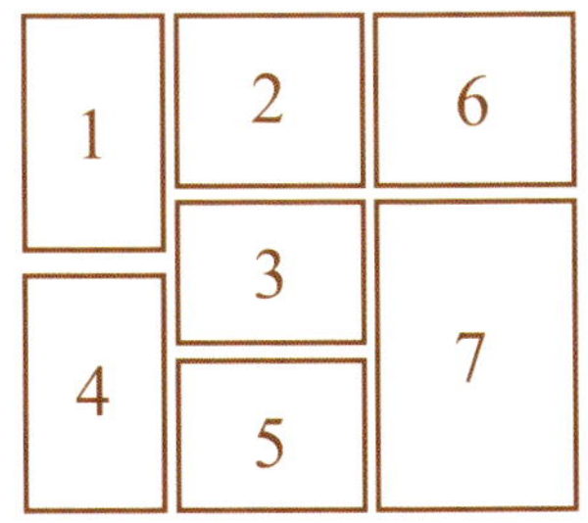

1. 1953年宋庆龄看望中国福利会托儿所的孩子们

2. 1955年6月宋庆龄在国际和平妇幼保健院看望产妇及婴儿

3. 1958年6月1日宋庆龄与中国福利会幼儿园的孩子们在上海寓所花园留影

4. 1960年1月27日宋庆龄、金仲华（左一）、李云（左三）等在中国福利会少年宫

5. 1964年5月10日宋庆龄在上海观看儿童艺术剧院演出《小足球队》后与演员合影

6. 宋庆龄与中国福利会的孩子们在一起

7. 1965年5月29日宋庆龄与巨鹿路第一小学乒乓球选手合影

Постановлением Комитета по международным СТАЛИНСКИМ премиям от 6 апреля 1951 года за выдающиеся заслуги в деле борьбы за сохранение и укрепление мира присуждена международная СТАЛИНСКАЯ премия „За укрепление мира между народами“

Сун Цзин-Лин

председателю Китайской ассоциации народной помощи

依據斯大林國際獎金委員會於一九五一年四月六日決定，爲表彰在保持及鞏固和平方面有卓越功績，特將「鞏固國際和平」斯大林國際獎金授予

中國人民救濟總會主席

宋慶齡

1951 年宋庆龄荣获“巩固国际和平”斯大林国际奖金的奖状和奖章

Certificate and Medal of Stalin Peace Prize awarded to Soong Ching Ling in 1951

● 1951 年 4 月 6 日，中国人民救济总会主席宋庆龄荣获 1950 年度“巩固国际和平”斯大林国际奖金，该奖金当年授予在维护与巩固和平的斗争中有卓越贡献的世界各国民主力量的代表 7 人。9 月 18 日，“巩固国际和平”斯大林国际奖金委员会在北京为宋庆龄举行了授奖典礼，由苏联作家伊里亚·格里戈里耶维奇·爱伦堡授予宋庆龄获奖证书和奖章。宋庆龄把 10 万卢布奖金捐赠中国福利会用于妇儿福利事业，在上海创建了国际和平妇幼保健院。

Statement of Soong Ching Ling on Winning the Stalin Peace Prize.

April 10,1951.

It is a most profound honor of my life to be named among the winners of the Stalin Peace Prize. It is a privilege to be associated with the fight for peace,with the name of Stalin. For peace is what the people of the world want most. And Stalin is the name which most personifies peace.

In accepting this most valued honor, I do so as a representative of the Chinese people. It has been their unrelenting revolutionary struggle which has placed the might of our nation on the side of peace. It has been their victory,in conjunction with the Socialist strides of the Soviet people and the courageous advances and stands of all other progressive elements, which has realigned the world for all time in favor of peace and people's rule.

The united front of all peoples today,continues at a most intensified pace the fight to maintain the peace. The monied moguls of the United States and its satellites,befouling the word"peace" by claiming to act in its behalf,are sustaining serious defeats. As a result they have become mad. They would mercilessly destroy all peaceful construction,as they have trampled into dust the achievements of the valiant Korean people. They would fiendishly tear child from mother or destroy both,as they are doing in Korea,Malaya and other parts of the world. They would strap all mankind to their exploitive service,to be reduced to slaves and cannon fodder,as they are attempting to do at home,in Western Germany and Japan. But they will never succeed in accomplishing their wicked ends,for the peoples united front for peace has its own special strength. Our hundreds if millions are pitted against their few,and as the World Peace Council demonstrates,there is not one sector ofthis earth where there is not representation and struggle for the aim of"consolidating peace among the nations".

Therefore,let us use thos occasion of the awarding of the Stalin Peace Prizes to rededicate ourselves in the cause of world peace. Let us gather new power and inspiration to defeat the enemies of man,to open the unparalleled vistas of peaceful work and joyful play that are man's due. Let us join in one voice to shout:

Long live Stalin,leader of the peoples for peace!
Long live the world peace forces!
Long live world peace!

Soong Ching Ling -

re-aligned
exploitive

1951 年 4 月宋庆龄文稿《为荣获“巩固国际和平”斯大林国际奖金而发表的谈话》

Statement of Soong Ching Ling on winning the Stalin Peace Prize in April 1951

● 1951 年 4 月 10 日，宋庆龄在上海寓所会见前来祝贺她荣获“巩固国际和平”斯大林国际奖金的中国人民保卫世界和平委员会上海分会的代表。宋庆龄除表示答谢外，还宣读了这份讲话稿，表示她“是以中国人民的一个代表来接受这个最高的荣誉的”，谴责美国好战分子“借口为和平而进行侵略”，“重申我们保卫世界和平而斗争的决心。让我们集合起新的力量，更加鼓舞起来战胜人类的敌人，创造人类应该获得和平地工作与愉快地生活的无比光明的前途”。

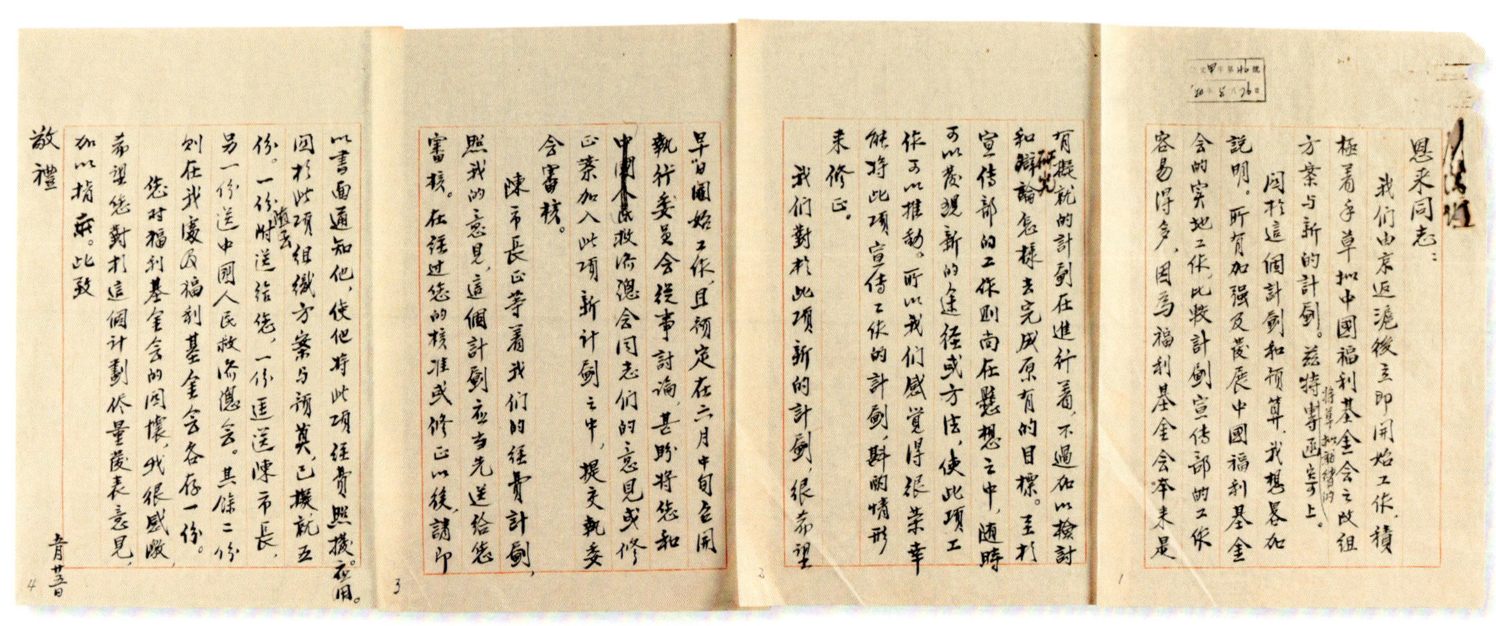

恩来同志：

我们由京返沪後立即开始工作，积极着手草拟中国福利基金会之改组方案与新的计划。兹特将草拟和预算的寄函上。

关于这个计划和预算，我想略加说明。所有加强及发展中国福利基金会的实地工作，比较计划宣传部的工作容易得多，因为福利基金会本来是有拟就的计划在进行着，不过加以检讨和研究怎样去完成原有的目标。至于宣传部的工作则尚在悬想之中，随时可以发现新的途径或方法，使此项工作可以推动。所以我们感觉得很荣幸能将此项宣传工作的计划，斟酌情形来修正。

我们对于此项新的计划，很希望早日开始工作，且预定在六月中旬召开执行委员会从事讨论，甚盼将您和中国人民救济总会同志们的意见或修正案加入此项新计划之中，提交执委会审核。

陈市长正等着我们的经费计划，照我们的意见，这个计划应当先送给您审核。在经过您的核准或修正以後，请即以书面通知他，使他将此项经费照拨应用。

关于此项组织方案与预算，已拟就五份。一份附送给您，一份转送陈市长，另一份送中国人民救济总会。其余二份则在我处及福利基金会各存一份。

您对福利基金会的关怀，我很感激，希望您对于这个计划尽量发表意见，加以指示。此致

敬礼

五月廿五日

1950 年 5 月 25 日宋庆龄致周恩来信

A letter from Soong Ching Ling to Zhou Enlai on May 25, 1950

● 1950 年，宋庆龄就中国福利基金会改组问题多次与周恩来通过函电讨论，此信中宋庆龄向周恩来汇报中国福利基金会改组的计划和预算情况。8 月，中国福利基金会正式改名为中国福利会。

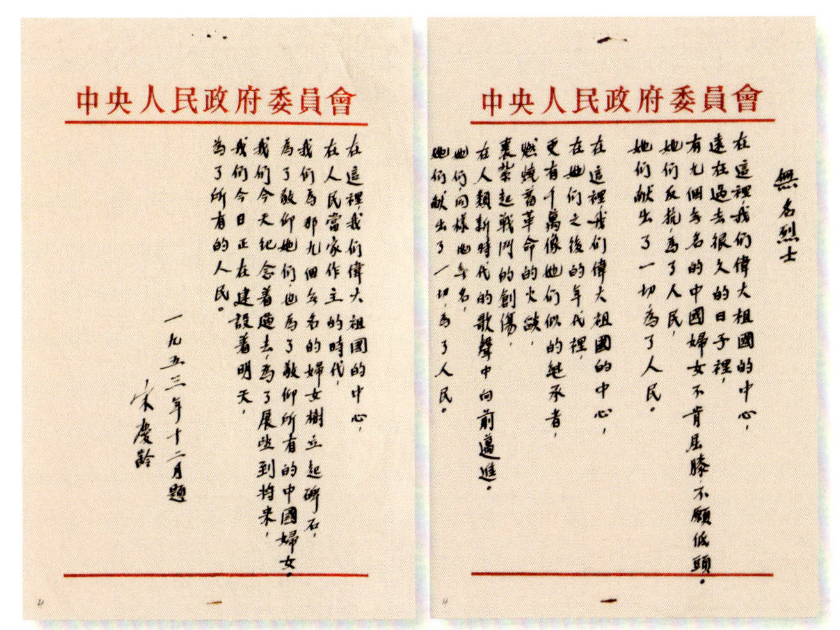

中央人民政府委員會

無名烈士

在這裡，我們偉大祖國的中心，
遠在過去很久的日子裡，
有九個無名的中國婦女不肯屈膝，不願低頭。
她們反抗，為了人民，
她們獻出了一切，為了人民。
在這裡，我們偉大祖國的中心，
在她們之後的年代裡，
更有千萬像她們似的繼承者，
燃燒着革命的火燄，
裹紮起戰鬥的創傷，
在人類新時代的歌聲中向前邁進。
她們同樣地無名，
她們獻出了一切，為了人民。

中央人民政府委員會

在這裡，我們偉大祖國的中心，
在人民當家作主的時代，
我們為那九個無名的婦女樹立起碑石，
為了敬仰她們，也為了敬仰所有的中國婦女。
我們今天紀念着過去，為了展望到將來，
我們今日正在建設着明天，
為了所有的人民。

一九五三年十二月題
宋慶齡

1953 年 12 月宋庆龄为武昌东湖九女墩撰写的《无名烈士》诗稿

The Nameless Martyrs, a poem written by Soong Ching Ling in December 1953, for the Nine-Women-Mound at the bank of East Lake in Wuchang

●相传清咸丰年间，清军镇压武昌的太平天国军队时，有女兵九人英勇抗击，全部壮烈牺牲。乡人将其遗骸合葬于武昌东湖边，时为避清廷迫害，特意将坟墓称为墩。1952 年，为纪念九位英勇就义的无名英雄，湖北武汉市人民政府将九女墩培土重修，建基立碑。1953 年 12 月，应中南行政委员会之请，宋庆龄撰写《无名烈士》诗稿，对九位烈士的大无畏精神给予了高度评价，并表达了对中国妇女的敬意：“我们为那九个无名的妇女树立起碑石，为了敬仰她们，也为了敬仰所有的中国妇女。”此诗后由何香凝书写后刻于碑的左侧，碑正面镌刻董必武撰写的《九女墩记》。

教育工作者，儿童工作者担负着侍候人的工作，担负着培育新的一代成为共产主义建设者和保卫者的工作。他们的产品是人，是共产主义新人，是祖国最宝贵的财富。这是一项光荣的任务，值得全社会的尊重。谨向侍候人的一侍候孩子的教育工作者和儿童工作者致敬！

宋庆龄

1958 年宋庆龄为教育工作者和儿童工作者题词

Soong Ching Ling's inscription for educators and childcare workers in 1958

● 1950 年，改组后的中国福利会致力于新中国妇幼卫生和儿童文化福利工作。1958 年 11 月 20 日，中国福利会执行委员会委员金仲华为了引起社会各方面对儿童工作者的重视，加强对儿童工作者的社会主义、共产主义教育，决定在《文汇报》上出版专页，他致信宋庆龄请她题词，宋庆龄欣然应允。题词表达了对教育工作者和儿童工作者的敬意。

欢 乐

春风吹开花蕾，
乐得咧开了嘴。
什么喜讯这样高兴？
咯咯笑声银铃般清脆。

快快说呀快快说，
让大家的心也快乐地飞。
——哈，知道了，知道了：
"六一"全班都入队。

马文忠 摄
查洪璧 诗

①

愿小树苗健康成长　宋庆龄

可爱的孩子们，每当我想到你们，我的眼前就浮现出那些充满生机的小树苗。你们象小树苗一样，柔软的枝条，嫩绿的叶子，在肥沃的土地上扎根，在和煦的阳光下成长。你们睁着惊奇的眼睛观察着：这个世界多么新鲜，多么有趣，多么灿烂！可是，我要提醒你们，狂风暴雨，病虫害，环境污染，都会危害小树的成长。对那些长得歪歪扭扭的小树，还要进行矫正、修剪。同样，社会上某些坏思想、坏风气和旧的习惯势力，也是对你们的危害和污染。因此，你们就需要认真学习，接受教育，增强抵抗力和提高辨别力。要学会在这个纷繁复杂、千变万化的世界上，辨别什么是真的，什么是假的；什么是美好的，什么是丑恶的；什么是正确的，什么是错误的。这样，你们就会象小树苗一样，长成大树，聚成森林，成为祖国需要的有用之材。

我国各族人民在中国共产党领导下，正在进行着社会主义现代化建设事业，这需要几十年时间和几代人的努力。你们是老一代开创的革命事业的接班人。再过一、二十年，你们将成为建设四化的主力军。你们要时刻准备着担负起这个光荣的任务。

我想，你们要在思想上、精神上作好准备。实现四个现代化，不但要有物质力量，还要有精神力量。什么是精神力量呢？要热爱社会主义祖国，继承光荣的革命传统；要有共产主义的远大理想，高尚的思想品德，助人为乐的精神和文明礼貌的行为。你们现在进行的"学雷锋、树新风"和"五讲"、"四美"活动就是这方面的起码的要求。希望你们从现在做起，从自己做起。

要刻苦学习文化科学知识。社会主义现代化要求我们要有高度的文化科学知识和聪明智慧。你们要通过学习，掌握古今中外的文化科学知识，并且要准备创造更高的文化科学。

要锻炼身体。要从小养成卫生习惯，保护眼睛，增强体质，才能获得充沛的精力，养成活泼开朗的性格。艰巨的工作在等待着你们，没有健康的身体是担当不起这个任务的。

还要有健康的文化艺术修养。对文学艺术要有鉴赏力，优美的音乐、美术、文学等对陶冶性情起着重要作用，能够抵制那些不健康的有害的东西，养成优美高尚的情操。

我们正在大力进行绿化祖国的工作，也正在对三亿以上少年儿童进行培养教育工作。我想象着葱绿的大地和鲜艳的红领巾将把祖国点缀得更加美丽多姿，更加欣欣向荣。愿你们和小树苗一同成长，成长得挺拔、旺盛，经得起任何暴风雨和病虫害的考验，成长为栋梁之材，成长为社会主义现代化建设事业的坚强接班人，为创造更高的物质文明和精神文明作出超过前人的巨大贡献。

· 1 ·

宋庆龄创办的《儿童时代》杂志

Children's Epoch, founded by Soong Ching Ling

● 1950 年 4 月，宋庆龄创办的《儿童时代》杂志出版，这是新中国第一份综合性儿童刊物。宋庆龄为杂志题写刊名并为创刊号题词，指明刊物的方针和任务。《儿童时代》面世后，宋庆龄多次为刊物精心撰文。1981 年 5 月 22 日，宋庆龄在《儿童时代》第 11 期上发表了人生最后一篇文章《愿小树苗健康成长》，热切期盼孩子们"成长为栋梁之材，成长为社会主义现代化建设事业的坚强接班人，为创造更高的物质文明和精神文明作出超过前人的巨大贡献"。

宋庆龄创办的《中国建设》杂志

China Reconstructs, founded by Soong Ching Ling

● 1952年1月，宋庆龄创办的《中国建设》英文双月刊在上海正式出版。这份杂志以报道中国的社会主义建设成就、人民生活的变化及新中国各方面背景知识，增进各国人民对中国人民的了解和友谊为办刊宗旨。1952年《中国建设》杂志的创刊号（左一），封面为土地改革中翻身农民的喜悦形象，封底为重建的钢铁基地鞍钢的木刻作品。创刊号上发表了宋庆龄的文章《世界和平与福利事业》以及陈翰笙、李德全、赵朴初等知名人士的文章。《中国建设》杂志出版后，又发行了多个语种，成为世界各国人民了解中国的重要窗口。宋庆龄极为喜爱《中国建设》杂志，经常将《中国建设》作为礼物送给国内外友人。《中国建设》1990年改名为《今日中国》，依然向世界讲述中国。

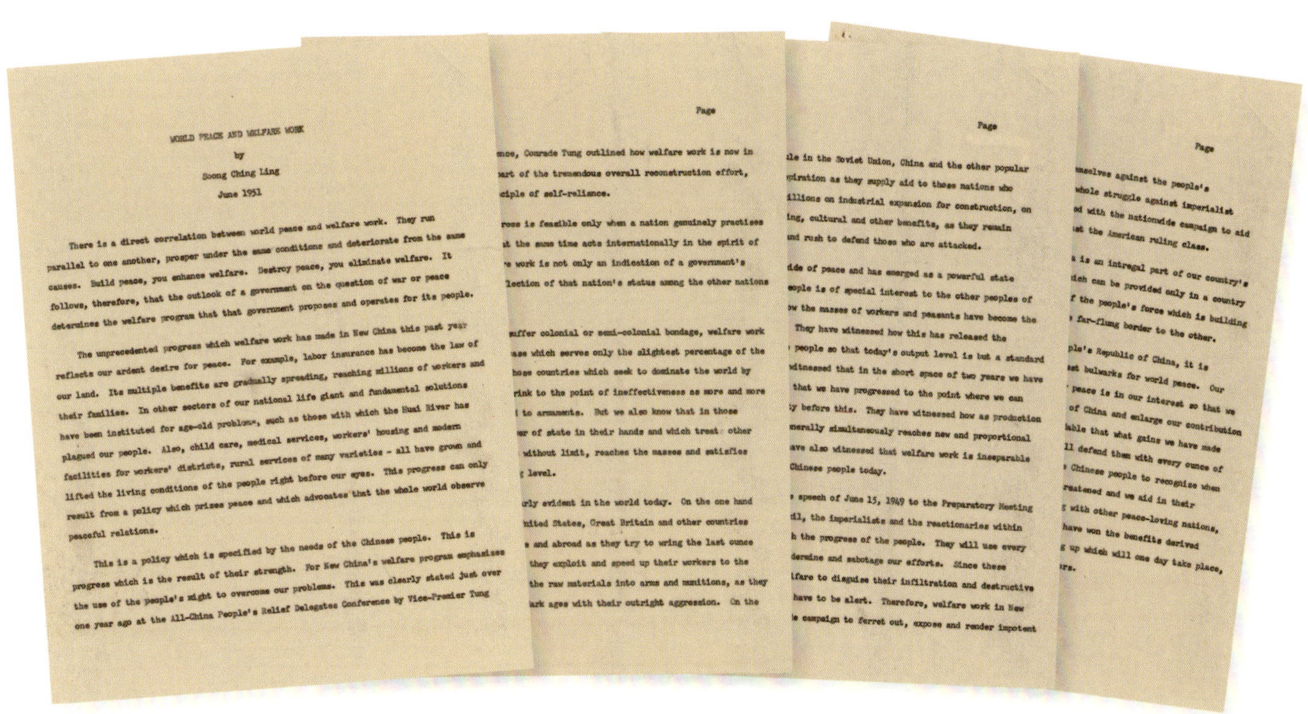

WORLD PEACE AND WELFARE WORK

by

Soong Ching Ling

June 1951

There is a direct correlation between world peace and welfare work. They run parallel to one another, prosper under the same conditions and deteriorate from the same causes. Build peace, you enhance welfare. Destroy peace, you eliminate welfare. It follows, therefore, that the outlook of a government on the question of war or peace determines the welfare program that that government proposes and operates for its people.

The unprecedented progress which welfare work has made in New China this past year reflects our ardent desire for peace. For example, labor insurance has become the law of our land. Its multiple benefits are gradually spreading, reaching millions of workers and their families. In other sectors of our national life giant and fundamental solutions have been instituted for age-old problems, such as those with which the Huai River has plagued our people. Also, child care, medical services, workers' housing and modern facilities for workers' districts, rural services of many varieties - all have grown and lifted the living conditions of the people right before our eyes. This progress can only result from a policy which prizes peace and which advocates that the whole world observe peaceful relations.

This is a policy which is specified by the needs of the Chinese people. This is progress which is the result of their strength. For New China's welfare program emphasizes the use of the people's might to overcome our problems. This was clearly stated just over one year ago at the All-China People's Relief Delegates Conference by Vice-Premier Tung

宋庆龄为《中国建设》创刊号撰写的《世界和平与福利事业》底稿

World Peace and Welfare Work written by Soong Ching Ling to the inaugural issue of *China Reconstructs*

●宋庆龄对《中国建设》杂志的创办倾注了大量的心血，亲自参与了杂志定名、编辑选定和编印发行等工作，并亲自为杂志撰写了30多篇文章。1951年6月，宋庆龄撰写《世界和平与福利事业》一文，发表在1952年1月出版的《中国建设》创刊号上，此件为文章底稿。文章阐明：“世界和平与福利事业有着直接的关联。两者是相辅而行的，可以在同样的条件下发展起来，也可以因同样的原因而受到危害。”“福利事业在新中国所表现的空前进步，反映了我们对于和平的热切愿望。”并指出中国是保卫世界和平的坚强堡垒。

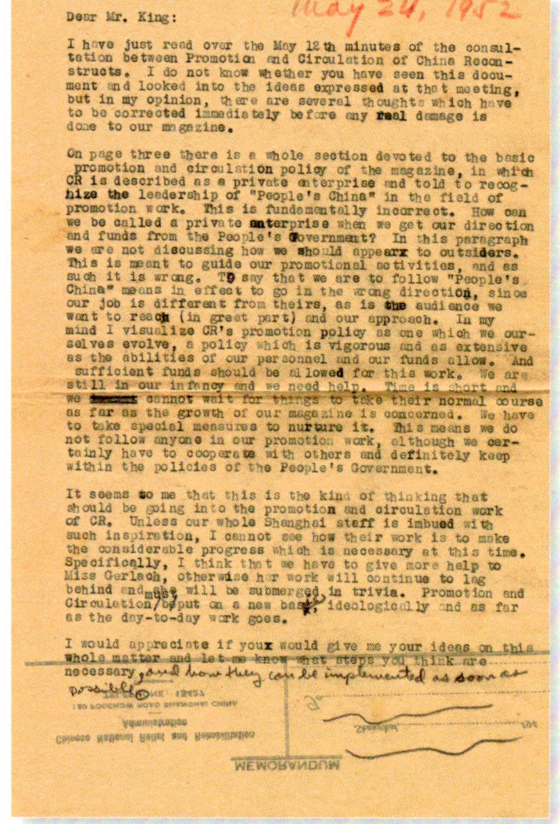

May 24, 1952

Dear Mr. King:

I have just read over the May 12th minutes of the consultation between Promotion and Circulation of China Reconstructs. I do not know whether you have seen this document and looked into the ideas expressed at that meeting, but in my opinion, there are several thoughts which have to be corrected immediately before any real damage is done to our magazine.

On page three there is a whole section devoted to the basic promotion and circulation policy of the magazine, in which CR is described as a private enterprise and told to recognize the leadership of "People's China" in the field of promotion work. This is fundamentally incorrect. How can we be called a private enterprise when we get our direction and funds from the People's Government? In this paragraph we are not discussing how we should appearx to outsiders. This is meant to guide our promotional activities, and as such it is wrong. To say that we are to follow "People's China" means in effect to go in the wrong direction, since our job is different from theirs, as is the audience we want to reach (in great part) and our approach. In my mind I visualize CR's promotion policy as one which we ourselves evolve, a policy which is vigorous and as extensive as the abilities of our personnel and our funds allow. And sufficient funds should be allowed for this work. We are still in our infancy and we need help. Time is short and we cannot wait for things to take their normal course as far as the growth of our magazine is concerned. We have to take special measures to nurture it. This means we do not follow anyone in our promotion work, although we certainly have to cooperate with others and definitely keep within the policies of the People's Government.

It seems to me that this is the kind of thinking that should be going into the promotion and circulation work of CR. Unless our whole Shanghai staff is imbued with such inspiration, I cannot see how their work is to make the considerable progress which is necessary at this time. Specifically, I think that we have to give more help to Miss Gerlach, otherwise her work will continue to lag behind and will be submerged in trivia. Promotion and Circulation must be put on a new basis, ideologically and as far as the day-to-day work goes.

I would appreciate if youx would give me your ideas on this whole matter and let me know what steps you think are necessary, and how they can be implemented as soon as possible.

1952年5月24日宋庆龄致金仲华信底稿

A letter from Soong Ching Ling to Jin Zhonghua on May 24, 1952

●信中宋庆龄与时任《中国建设》杂志社社长的金仲华商议《中国建设》的宣传推广和发行工作，指出必须立即纠正《中国建设》宣传推广部门和发行部门会议记录中的部分观点，强调《中国建设》的宣传推广不跟从任何人，应在人员能力和经费允许范围内尽可能制定有力而广泛的宣传推广政策。信函底稿上方有宋庆龄手写的“May 24, 1952”（1952年5月24日）字样，另有多处修改痕迹。

1962 年 1 月宋庆龄与周恩来、陈毅等出席《中国建设》创刊十周年招待会

Soong Ching Ling with Zhou Enlai, Chen Yi and others attending the reception for the 10th anniversary of the founding of *China Reconstructs* in January 1962

● 1962 年 1 月 6 日，宋庆龄与周恩来、陈毅等出席《中国建设》创刊十周年招待会，并参观该杂志社举办的展览会。之后，宋庆龄与周恩来、陈毅、邓颖超等前往《中国建设》编辑部，接见全社工作人员及外国专家并同他们合影留念。前排左起：周恩来、爱泼斯坦、李伯悌，前排左五：黄浣碧，二排左一：金仲华，二排左四：邱茉莉，二排左九：邓颖超，二排左十一：宋庆龄，二排左十三：陈毅，二排左十六：唐明照，二排左十七：耿丽淑。

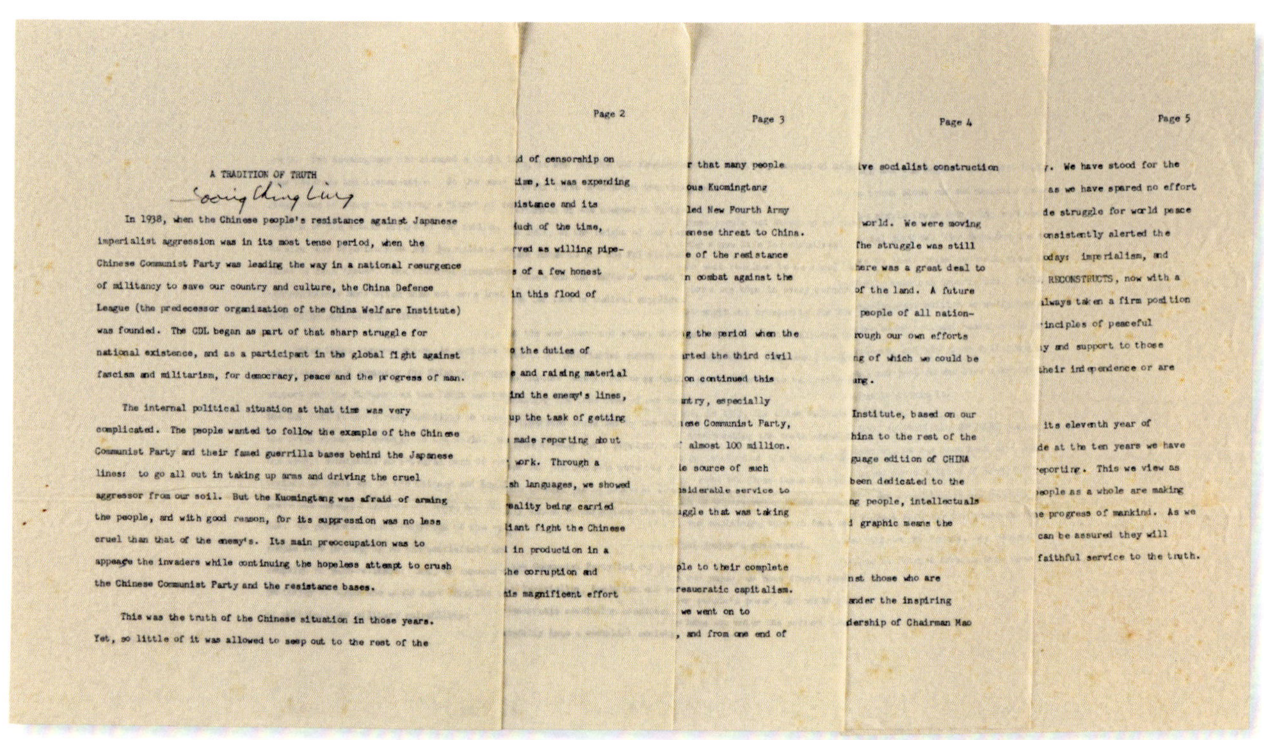

A TRADITION OF TRUTH

Soong Ching Ling

In 1938, when the Chinese people's resistance against Japanese imperialist aggression was in its most tense period, when the Chinese Communist Party was leading the way in a national resurgence of militancy to save our country and culture, the China Defence League (the predecessor organization of the China Welfare Institute) was founded. The CDL began as part of that sharp struggle for national existence, and as a participant in the global fight against fascism and militarism, for democracy, peace and the progress of man.

The internal political situation at that time was very complicated. The people wanted to follow the example of the Chinese Communist Party and their famed guerrilla bases behind the Japanese lines: to go all out in taking up arms and driving the cruel aggressor from our soil. But the Kuomingtang was afraid of arming the people, and with good reason, for its suppression was no less cruel than that of the enemy's. Its main preoccupation was to appease the invaders while continuing the hopeless attempt to crush the Chinese Communist Party and the resistance bases.

This was the truth of the Chinese situation in those years. Yet, so little of it was allowed to seep out to the rest of the

Page 2

d of censorship on
ime, it was expending
sistance and its
Much of the time,
rved as willing pipe-
s of a few honest
in this flood of

o the duties of
e and raising material
ind the enemy's lines,
up the task of getting
made reporting about
work. Through a
sh languages, we showed
reality being carried
iant fight the Chinese
l in production in a
he corruption and
is magnificent effort

Page 3

r that many people
ous Kuomingtang
led New Fourth Army
nese threat to China.
e of the resistance
n combat against the

g the period when the
rted the third civil
on continued this
ntry, especially
ese Communist Party,
almost 100 million.
e source of such
siderable service to
ggle that was taking

ple to their complete
reaucratic capitalism.
we went on to
, and from one end of

Page 4

ive socialist construction

world. We were moving
The struggle was still
here was a great deal to
of the land. A future
people of all nation-
rough our own efforts
ng of which we could be
ng.

Institute, based on our
hina to the rest of the
guage edition of CHINA
been dedicated to the
ng people, intellectuals
d graphic means the

nst those who are
nder the inspiring
dership of Chairman Mao

Page 5

y. We have stood for the
as we have spared no effort
de struggle for world peace
onsistently alerted the
oday: imperialism, and
RECONSTRUCTS, now with a
lways taken a firm position
inciples of peaceful
y and support to those
their independence or are

its eleventh year of
de at the ten years we have
eporting. This we view as
eople as a whole are making
e progress of mankind. As we
can be assured they will
faithful service to the truth.

宋庆龄为庆祝《中国建设》创刊十周年撰写的文稿《真实报道的传统》

A Tradition of Truth written by Soong Ching Ling to celebrate the 10th anniversary of the founding of *China Reconstructs*

●《真实报道的传统》是宋庆龄为《中国建设》杂志创刊十周年而撰写的文章。她在文章中再次强调创刊的宗旨并回顾说："在一九五二年，中国福利会开始出版英文版的《中国建设》来继承并发扬它的前身保卫中国同盟所建立的、向世界各地传播中国的真实情况的优良传统。这个刊物从创办伊始，就一直致力于描述我国劳动人民、知识分子和文艺工作者的成就，并且通过具体事实和形象化的报道来阐明人民政府的政策。" "我们可以自豪地回顾过去的十年。在这段时期里，我们保持了真实报道的传统。我们把这一点看成是全体中国人民对于争取和平与人类进步的伟大斗争所作的贡献的一部分。"并表示：当第二个十年开始的时候，"我们将同过去一样，忠诚地为真理效劳"。这篇文章发表于1962年第1期《中国建设》上。

1952 年 10 月宋庆龄在亚洲及太平洋区域和平会议上致开幕词

Soong Ching Ling delivering opening speech at the Peace Conference of the Asian and Pacific Regions in October 1952

● 1952 年 10 月，亚洲及太平洋区域和平会议在北京召开，宋庆龄率中国代表团出席会议，担任会议执行主席并致开幕词。在会上宋庆龄当选为亚洲及太平洋区域和平联络委员会主席。

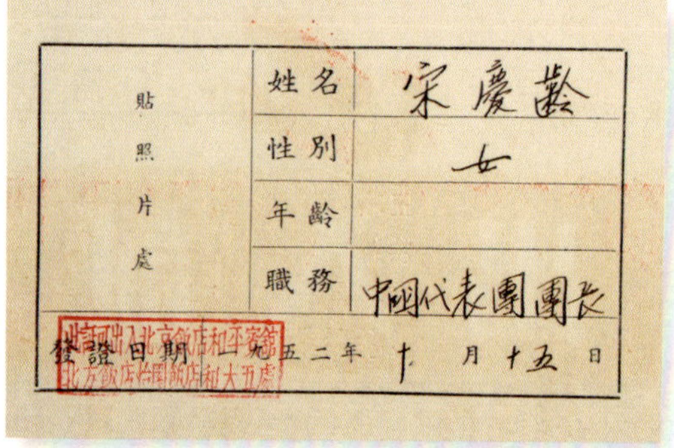

貼照片處	姓名	宋慶齡
	性別	女
	年齡	
	職務	中国代表團團長

發證日期 一九五二年 十 月 十五 日

1952 年 10 月宋庆龄参加亚洲及太平洋区域和平会议时使用的文件夹和出席亚洲及太平洋区域和平联络委员会成立会议的出入证

Soong Ching Ling's folder for the Peace Conference of the Asian and Pacific Regions and her admission certificate for the Peace Conference Committee of the Asian and Pacific Regions in October 1952

●文件夹上方图案为西班牙画家毕加索 1950 年为第二届世界保卫和平大会绘制的和平鸽，下有中、俄、英、法四国语言的“亚洲及太平洋区域和平会议”和“北京”字样。出入证上印有“特字第 00217 号”字样，反面写有“宋庆龄”“女”字样，职务为“中国代表团团长”，发证日期为“一九五二年十月十五日”。宋庆龄于当日主持亚洲及太平洋区域和平联络委员会成立会议并致辞。

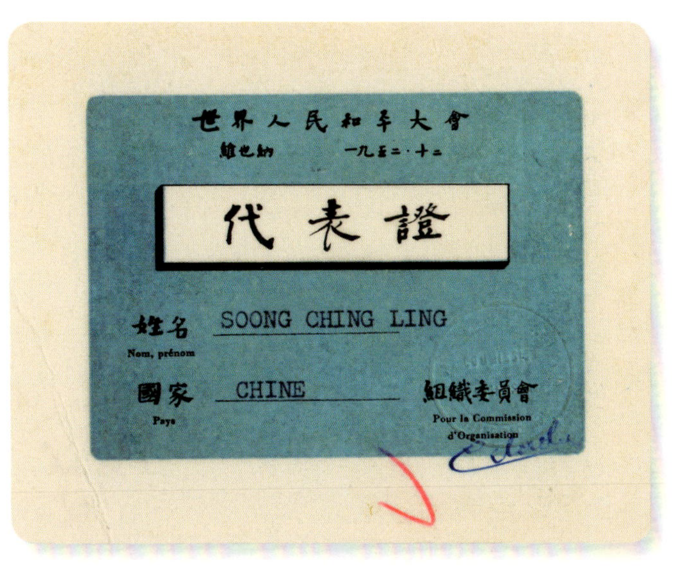

1952年12月宋庆龄参加维也纳世界人民和平大会的代表证和徽章

Soong Ching Ling's representative certificate and badge for the World Peace Conference in Vienna in December 1952

● 1952年12月，宋庆龄率领中国代表团出席在维也纳召开的世界人民和平大会，被推选为会议执行主席。代表证为宋庆龄参加大会时所用，上印有“SOONG CHING LING”（宋庆龄）和“CHINE”（中国）字样，反面印有编号“3210”。

中华人民共和国成立后，宋庆龄作为国家领导人接待了许多国家元首和外国代表团，并多次出国访问，为新中国架起了和平友谊的桥梁

After the birth of the People's Republic of China, Soong Ching Ling, as a major leader of the country, received many heads of State and foreign delegations, paid a number of visits abroad and helped the new China to build bridge of friendship across nations

1.1957年11月16日，宋庆龄随同毛泽东参加在莫斯科举行的社会主义国家共产党和工人党代表会议宣言的签字仪式。毛泽东在宣言上签字时，宋庆龄和邓小平分别坐在他的两边。

2.1957年9月25日宋庆龄在上海寓所会见印度副总统萨瓦帕利·拉达克里希南

3.1956年10月11日宋庆龄在上海寓所会见印度尼西亚总统艾哈迈德·苏加诺

4.1957年4月24日宋庆龄在上海寓所设宴欢迎苏联最高苏维埃主席团主席克利缅特·叶夫列莫维奇·伏罗希洛夫（左二）

5.1964年2月27日宋庆龄出访锡兰时和锡兰总理西丽玛沃·班达拉奈克夫人在科伦坡市郊

6.1963年2月20日宋庆龄在上海寓所会见柬埔寨国家元首诺罗敦·西哈努克亲王（左二）

7.1956年5月11日宋庆龄在上海寓所花园设茶会招待出席国际民主妇女联合会理事会的24国妇女代表

8.1955年12月16日宋庆龄出访印度时在新德里巴兰机场受到总理贾瓦哈拉尔·尼赫鲁（右一）等人的欢迎

苏联友人赠送宋庆龄的十月革命胜利 40 周年纪念瓷盘

The porcelain plate marking the 40th anniversary of the victory of the October Revolution, a present to Soong Ching Ling from the Soviet friends

● 1957 年 11 月，宋庆龄随毛泽东带领的中国代表团访问苏联，参加苏联十月革命胜利 40 周年庆典以及同时在莫斯科举行的社会主义国家共产党和工人党代表会议。宋庆龄回国时带回了苏联友人赠送的庆祝十月革命胜利 40 周年的纪念品，此件纪念瓷盘是其中之一。瓷盘中“40”下方的俄文字意依次为“周年”“十月”。

印度驻华大使内德亚姆·赖嘉文赠送宋庆龄的银盘

A silver plate presented to Soong Ching Ling by Nedyam Raghavan, Indian Ambassador to China

●银盘为镂空花卉形状，八瓣四足。银盘中央刻有宋庆龄的英文名字缩写 SCL，背面刻有英文“赖嘉文赠”（FROM RAGHAVAN）。赖嘉文为印度第二任驻华大使。

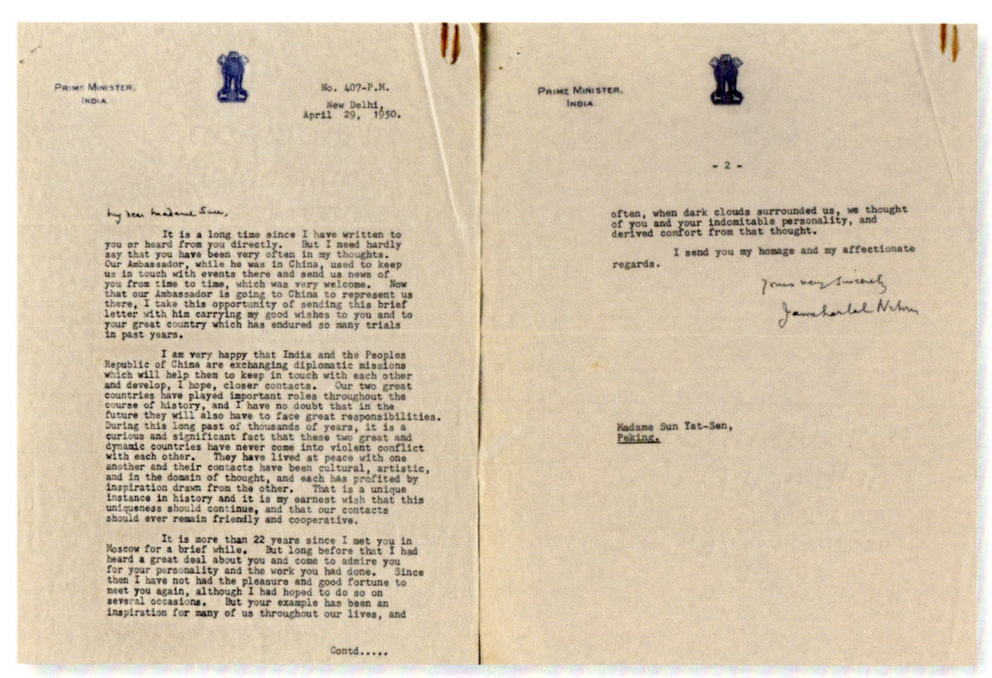

PRIME MINISTER,
INDIA.

No. 407-P.M.

New Delhi,
April 29, 1950.

My dear Madame Sun,

It is a long time since I have written to you or heard from you directly. But I need hardly say that you have been very often in my thoughts. Our Ambassador, while he was in China, used to keep us in touch with events there and send us news of you from time to time, which was very welcome. Now that our Ambassador is going to China to represent us there, I take this opportunity of sending this brief letter with him carrying my good wishes to you and to your great country which has endured so many trials in past years.

I am very happy that India and the Peoples Republic of China are exchanging diplomatic missions which will help them to keep in touch with each other and develop, I hope, closer contacts. Our two great countries have played important roles throughout the course of history, and I have no doubt that in the future they will also have to face great responsibilities. During this long past of thousands of years, it is a curious and significant fact that these two great and dynamic countries have never come into violent conflict with each other. They have lived at peace with one another and their contacts have been cultural, artistic, and in the domain of thought, and each has profited by inspiration drawn from the other. That is a unique instance in history and it is my earnest wish that this uniqueness should continue, and that our contacts should ever remain friendly and cooperative.

It is more than 22 years since I met you in Moscow for a brief while. But long before that I had heard a great deal about you and come to admire you for your personality and the work you had done. Since then I have not had the pleasure and good fortune to meet you again, although I had hoped to do so on several occasions. But your example has been an inspiration for many of us throughout our lives, and

Contd.....

PRIME MINISTER,
INDIA.

- 2 -

often, when dark clouds surrounded us, we thought of you and your indomitable personality, and derived comfort from that thought.

I send you my homage and my affectionate regards.

Yours very sincerely
Jawaharlal Nehru

Madame Sun Yat-Sen,
Peking.

1950 年 4 月 29 日印度总理贾瓦哈拉尔·尼赫鲁致宋庆龄信

A letter from Indian Prime Minister Jawaharlal Nehru to Soong Ching Ling on April 29, 1950

●宋庆龄与贾瓦哈拉尔·尼赫鲁 1927 年于苏联相识，此后长期保持书信联系。此件为 1950 年 4 月 29 日印度总理尼赫鲁致宋庆龄信，彼时中印两国刚刚建交，正在互派外交使团，尼赫鲁借印度驻华大使到中国上任的机会捎去此信，表达对宋庆龄和中国的良好祝愿。信中希望两国良好的关系保持下去，在友谊和合作的基础上继续建立交往，尼赫鲁还写道："您一直是鼓舞我们前进的榜样。有时，当阴云笼罩着我们时，我们就会想起您，想起您不屈不挠的个性并从中获得安慰。"信件起首有尼赫鲁书写的"My Dear Madame Sun"（亲爱的孙夫人）字样，信尾落亲笔署名。

1956 年 10 月巴基斯坦总理侯赛恩·沙希德·苏拉瓦底赠送宋庆龄的银錾花掐丝嵌珠宝烟盒
The silver cigarette box presented to Soong Ching Ling by Pakistani Prime Minister Huseyn Shaheed Suhrawardy in October 1956

● 1956 年 10 月 27 日，宋庆龄在上海淮海中路寓所设宴招待巴基斯坦总理苏拉瓦底。苏拉瓦底将这只银烟盒赠送宋庆龄，宋庆龄回赠了福建漆制茶具和中国茶叶。银烟盒正中为菱形宝石图案，周边饰有掐丝叶纹和花卉纹，嵌有多粒珍珠、红绿宝石，四矮足，足面刻五条棱纹。

1956年宋庆龄受赠的迦楼罗木雕彩绘

A painted Garuda wood carving presented to Soong Ching Ling in 1956

● 1956年8月，宋庆龄出访印度尼西亚时受赠此件迦楼罗木雕彩绘。迦楼罗是古印度神话传说中记载的一种巨型神鸟，在印度教中是三大主神之一毗湿奴的坐骑，在佛教中是天龙八部(守护佛教的诸天和龙神等八部的合称)之一，以龙为食。印度尼西亚将迦楼罗视作力量和忠心的象征。这座迦楼罗木雕色彩鲜艳，形象为半人半鸟，生有鹰首、利爪和喙，双翅高展，身躯和四肢与人相同，具有浓郁的东南亚特色。

1962 年墨西哥前总统拉萨罗·卡德纳斯赠送宋庆龄的拼花木盒

A wooden mosaic box presented to Soong Ching Ling by the former Mexican President Lazaro Cardenas in 1962

● 1962 年 8 月，墨西哥和平委员会主席吉列尔莫·蒙塔尼奥博士来华访问时，受墨西哥前总统拉萨罗·卡德纳斯将军之托，将此拼花木盒赠送给宋庆龄。宋庆龄与卡德纳斯均为世界和平委员会领导成员。1959 年 1 月 24 日，宋庆龄曾在上海淮海中路寓所会见卡德纳斯将军。

1963 年锡兰总理西丽玛沃·班达拉奈克夫人赠送宋庆龄的银錾花首饰盒

An engraved silver jewelry box presented to Soong Ching Ling in 1963 by Mrs. Sirimavo Bandaranaike, Prime Minister of Ceylon

● 1963 年 1 月 7 日，宋庆龄在上海淮海中路寓所会晤来访的锡兰总理西丽玛沃·班达拉奈克夫人，宋庆龄赠送给班达拉奈克夫人一本《中国建设》杂志，班达拉奈克夫人将此银錾花首饰盒赠送给宋庆龄。班达拉奈克夫人还热情邀请宋庆龄、周恩来在方便时访问锡兰。银盒饰有锡兰特色的象纹、狮纹和花卉纹等纹饰，四足。锡兰今称斯里兰卡，1957 年与中国建交。

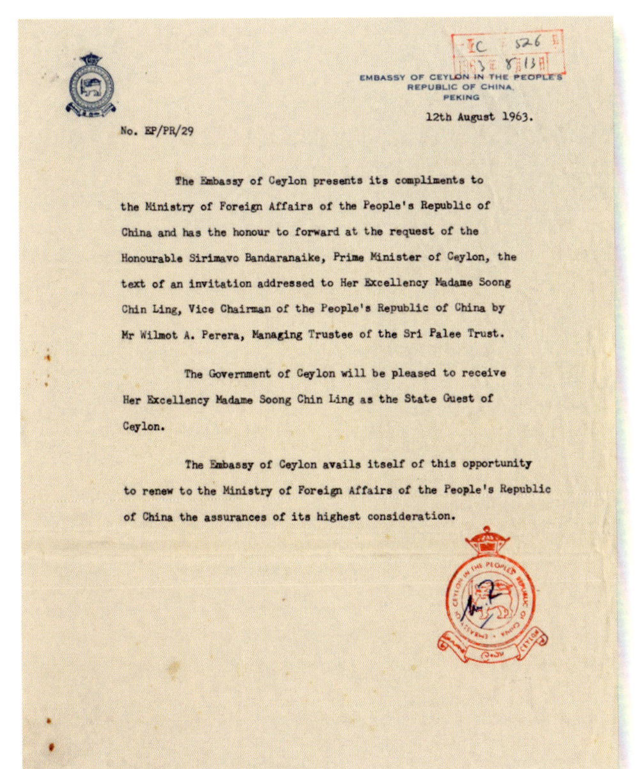

EMBASSY OF CEYLON IN THE PEOPLE'S REPUBLIC OF CHINA. PEKING

12th August 1963.

No. EP/PR/29

The Embassy of Ceylon presents its compliments to the Ministry of Foreign Affairs of the People's Republic of China and has the honour to forward at the request of the Honourable Sirimavo Bandaranaike, Prime Minister of Ceylon, the text of an invitation addressed to Her Excellency Madame Soong Chin Ling, Vice Chairman of the People's Republic of China by Mr Wilmot A. Perera, Managing Trustee of the Sri Palee Trust.

The Government of Ceylon will be pleased to receive Her Excellency Madame Soong Chin Ling as the State Guest of Ceylon.

The Embassy of Ceylon avails itself of this opportunity to renew to the Ministry of Foreign Affairs of the People's Republic of China the assurances of its highest consideration.

译 文

1963 年 8 月 12 日

锡兰大使馆向中华人民共和国外交部致意，并谨应锡兰总理西丽玛沃·班达拉奈克阁下的要求转交司丽巴利组织董事长威尔莫特·爱·佩雷拉先生给中华人民共和国副主席宋庆龄夫人阁下的邀请信。

锡兰政府将愉快地来接待锡兰的国宾宋庆龄夫人阁下。

顺致最崇高的敬意。

（锡兰驻中华人民共和国大使馆章）

1963 年 8 月 12 日锡兰驻华使馆致中国外交部的照会

The diplomatic note sent by the Embassy of Ceylon in the People's Republic of China on August 12, 1963

●照会由锡兰驻华使馆发出，表达了锡兰总理班达拉奈克夫人邀请中华人民共和国副主席宋庆龄作为国宾访问锡兰的诚恳意愿。1964 年 2 月，中华人民共和国副主席宋庆龄应邀访问锡兰，国务院总理周恩来，国务院副总理、外交部长陈毅陪同出访。

1961 年 7 月朝鲜民主主义人民共和国党政代表团赠送宋庆龄的漆盒

A lacquer box presented to Soong Ching Ling by the party and government delegation of the Democratic People's Republic of Korea in July 1961

● 1961 年 7 月，朝鲜劳动党中央委员会委员长、朝鲜民主主义人民共和国内阁首相金日成率领朝鲜党政代表团来华访问并签订《中朝友好合作互助条约》，此件为朝鲜民主主义人民共和国党政代表团访华期间赠送宋庆龄的嵌贝漆盒。漆盒由秦川漆制成，耐热、耐湿、耐酸碱和防腐。盒面光亮润滑，以螺钿嵌成木槿花图案。礼盒是秦川漆器的代表作。

捷克斯洛伐克友人赠送宋庆龄的车料玻璃花瓶

A cut glass vase presented to Soong Ching Ling by the friends of Czechoslovakia

波兰友人赠送宋庆龄的车料玻璃果盆

A cut glass fruit bowl presented to Soong Ching Ling by the friends of Poland

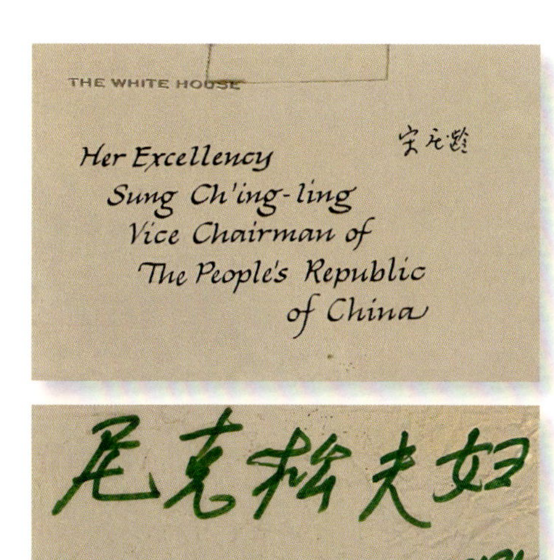

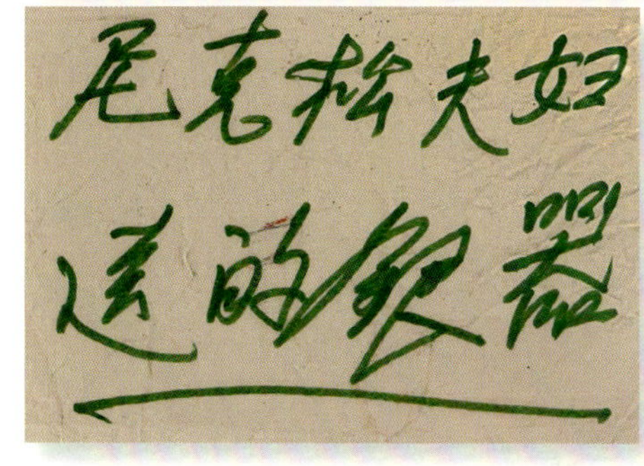

1972 年美国总统理查德·米尔豪斯·尼克松赠送宋庆龄的银质餐具

Silverwares presented to Soong Ching Ling by the US President Richard Milhous Nixon in 1972

● 1972 年 2 月 21 日至 28 日，美国总统理查德·米尔豪斯·尼克松在访华期间，将此银质餐具赠送给宋庆龄。一套四件，由盘、碗组成。盘中央饰有美国总统徽记，由美国蒂芙尼公司制造。随附一张卡片上印有“THE WHITE HOUSE Her Excellency Sung Ch'ing-Ling Vice Chairman of The People's Republic of China”（白宫 尊敬的宋庆龄阁下 中华人民共和国副主席），并写有“宋庆龄”中文名字；一张便条为宋庆龄亲笔所书“尼克松夫妇送的银器”。

MÁ VLAST
MY COUNTRY
SUPRAPHON
CARMEN
PIANO MUSIC
OF
DEBUSSY

宋庆龄曾说，去北京是上班，回上海则是回家，她把这里称为“可爱的家”。她在给友人的信中写道：“我刚刚到家，发现气候清爽，我很喜欢……我的小花园很怡人，有高大桉（樟）树，鸟儿在上面筑巢，清晨鸟儿们歌唱。我的管家说它们似乎知道我回家了，一直在歌唱！”

Soong Ching Ling once said, Beijing was the place where she worked but Shanghai was where she lived, as she called it “a lovely home”. In a letter to her friend, she wrote: “I have just arrived at my home and find the climate just bracing and to my liking. …My little garden here is lovely with tall eucalyptus (camphor) trees where birds make their nests and singing all the morning. My home-keeper says they seem to know that I've returned home, for they sing now all the time!”

1957 年宋庆龄在上海淮海中路寓所客厅

Soong Ching Ling in her residence in Middle Huaihai Road in Shanghai in 1957

宋庆龄收藏的木狮摆件

A wooden lion ornament preserved by Soong Ching Ling

宋庆龄酷爱读书，她曾说："我最大的乐趣就是阅读可以找到的各种杂志和书籍"，故居保存了数千册她的藏书，内容涵盖文学、政治、法律等多个领域，涉及中、英、日、俄等多个语种

Soong Ching Ling loved reading. She once said: "I've derived great pleasure from reading various magazines and books within my reach." Soong Ching Ling Memorial Residence houses thousands of books, covering literary, politics, laws and other fields in different languages such as Chinese, English, Japanese and Russian

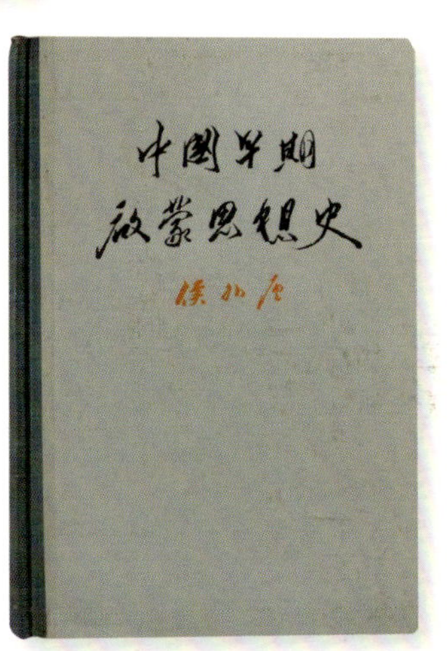

宋庆龄的部分藏书

Books preserved by Soong Ching Ling

●受教育背景影响，宋庆龄深嗜西洋文学，在书信中常会引用查尔斯·狄更斯等人的作品，《大卫·科波菲尔》、《莎士比亚戏剧全集》(1927 年)、《巴黎圣母院》、《沃尔特·司各特小说集》等西方经典文学作品，展示了宋庆龄的阅读偏好。《音乐史》《电影图史》《毕加索画册》等风格各异的图书，反映了宋庆龄对艺术的喜爱。宋庆龄还保存了大量中文图书，从《马克思传》（1956 年）、《中国早期启蒙思想史》（1956 年）等亦能瞥见宋庆龄的阅读范围和兴趣。

宋庆龄收藏的部分唱片

Music records preserved by Soong Ching Ling

●宋庆龄自幼接受西方音乐教育，钟爱贝多芬、海顿、柴可夫斯基、瓦格纳、莫扎特等音乐家的创作，对歌剧、交响曲、协奏曲、奏鸣曲等各种表现形态的作品都很喜欢。《贝多芬第五交响曲》、歌剧《卡门》选段、《德彪西钢琴曲》反映了她对古典音乐的钟情。宋庆龄对音乐有自己的欣赏力和感悟力，她特别珍藏着捷克作曲家斯美塔那创作的交响诗《我的祖国》唱片，在聆听宏伟瑰丽的乐曲声中寄托自己的爱国热情。《梁山伯与祝英台》《黄河大合唱》等中国当代优秀音乐作品展示了宋庆龄对中国乐曲的关注。

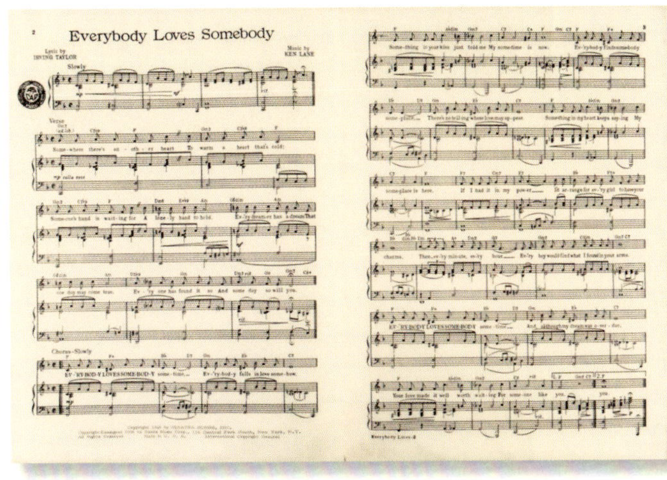

宋庆龄收藏的歌谱

Song sheets preserved by Soong Ching Ling

●《雪中幸运》(*Fortune in Snow*)为苏格兰圣诞短歌，歌谱由词曲作者弗兰克·伊佐题赠宋庆龄，内页写有“Best Regards From Frankie”（来自弗兰克的最好祝福）。歌谱1963年由美国康涅狄格州诺斯黑文市的多佛音乐出版社出版。《每个人都有心中所爱》(*Everybody Loves Somebody*)歌谱，1966年10月15日由韩·帕帝题赠宋庆龄。歌谱由欧文·泰勒作词，肯·兰恩作曲，由美国纽约金沙音乐制作公司出版。

宋庆龄用过的打火机和烟盒

A lighter and a cigarette case used by Soong Ching Ling

●打火机为朗森牌（RONSON）定制款打火机，刻有宋庆龄英文名字（Soong Ching Ling）缩写“SCL”，由美国新泽西州纽瓦克市生产。

宋庆龄戴过的手表

A watch used by Soong Ching Ling

●此件为瑞士出产的莱斯牌（ROYCE）手表，防水抗震，钢制表背，为17钻普通功能手表，编号11528。

宋庆龄的首饰和化妆品

Ornaments and cosmetics used by Soong Ching Ling

宋庆龄穿过的旗袍和西装套裙

The cheongsam and suit skirt worn by Soong Ching Ling

宋庆龄用过的手袋，SCL 为宋庆龄英文名字缩写
A handbag used by Soong Ching Ling, SCL is abbreviation of Soong Ching Ling

1964 年沈粹缜和黎沛华等写的联句

The couplet written by Shen Cuizhen, Li Peihua and others in 1964

●每逢节日，宋庆龄经常邀请朋友、工作人员及其家人到家中欢聚。1964 年 1 月 1 日，时任国家副主席的宋庆龄邀请工作人员子女前来北京寓所欢度元旦，一起打红蝴蝶结，并观看了工作人员及其子女们的娱乐游戏。此件即为沈粹缜［曾任中国福利基金会（中国福利会）托儿所所长］和黎沛华（曾任宋庆龄秘书）等人根据当时大家的游戏场景所写的联句，联句内容为：“宋付（副）主席和大家一起欢度元旦佳节，即景志念。六十多岁的老人带头做游戏，来一个老鹰捉小鸡，缜做鹰来华做鸡，后面拖了一群小把戏，乐得大家喘不上气，真有趣呀真有趣！”

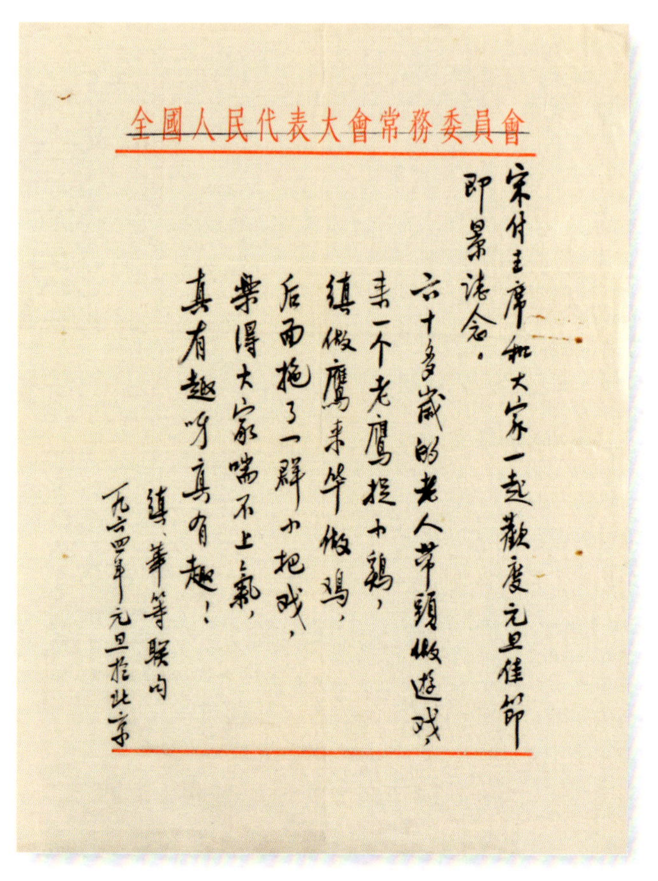
全國人民代表大會常務委員會

宋付主席和大家一起歡度元旦佳節
即景誌念。
六十多歲的老人帶頭做遊戏，
来一个老鷹捉小鷄，
缜做鷹来华做鷄，
后面拖了一群小把戏，
樂得大家喘不上氣，
真有趣呀真有趣！
缜、华等联句
一九六四年元旦於北京

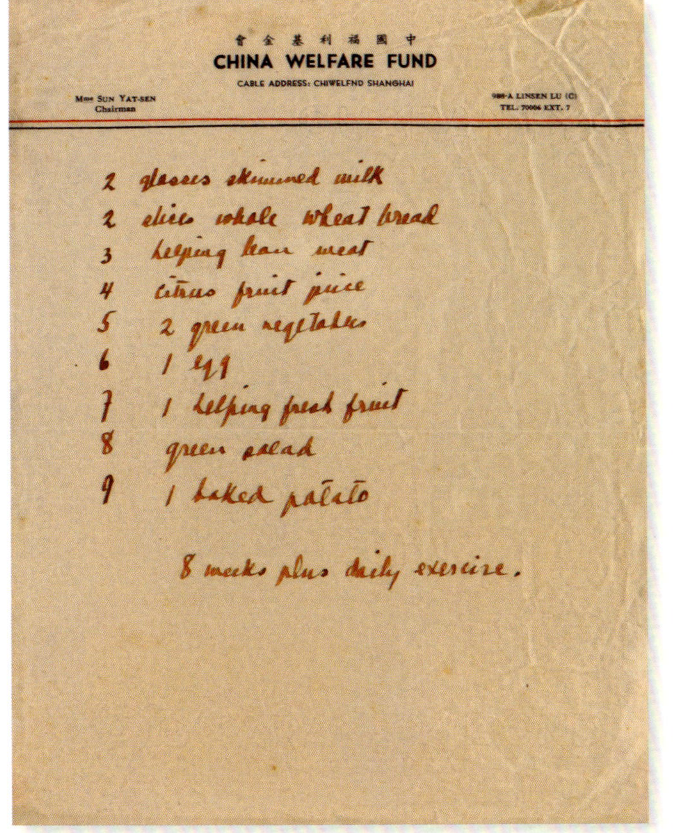

中國福利基金會

CHINA WELFARE FUND

CABLE ADDRESS: CHIWELFND SHANGHAI

Mme SUN YAT-SEN
Chairman

988-A LINSEN LU (C)
TEL. 70006 EXT. 7

2 glasses skimmed milk
2 slices whole wheat bread
3 helping lean meat
4 citrus fruit juice
5 2 green vegetables
6 1 egg
7 1 helping fresh fruit
8 green salad
9 1 baked potato

8 weeks plus daily exercise.

宋庆龄为自己制定的健康食谱

The healthy recipe made by Soong Ching Ling

●宋庆龄的饮食习惯受中西两种文化的影响，在美国留学的经历让她养成西式的用餐习惯。此件食谱中，宋庆龄为自己规定了“两杯牛奶、两片白面包、一客火腿肉、橙汁、两种绿叶蔬菜、一个鸡蛋、一客水果、蔬菜沙拉和烤土豆”等食品，并写有“八周加上每天锻炼”的字样。食谱既注重饮食的营养搭配，又重视运动锻炼，展示了宋庆龄健康的生活方式。食谱写于“中国福利基金会”的信纸上。

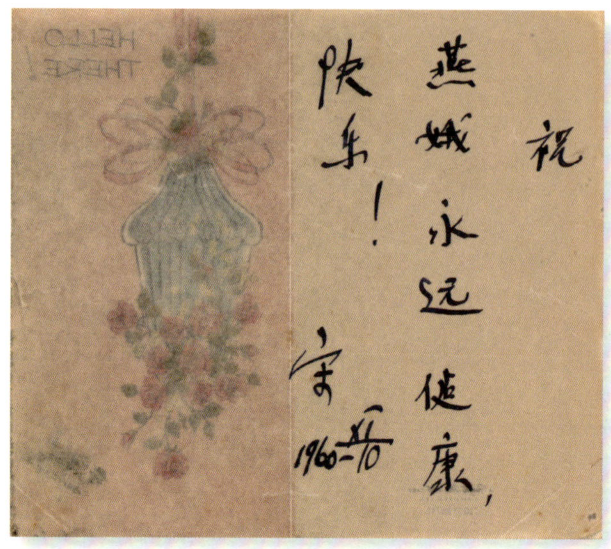

宋庆龄与友人互赠的贺卡

Greeting cards exchanged between Soong Ching Ling and her friends

●宋庆龄注重友情，节假日总与友人互赠贺卡，表达问候。上排左一为宋庆龄送给沈粹缜的贺卡（邹嘉骊捐赠），热情地称呼她为“亲爱的沈大姐”。上排左二为宋庆龄送给保姆李燕娥的贺卡，写着：“祝燕娥永远健康，快乐！”上排右一为宋庆龄送给生活管理员周和康的贺卡（周和康捐赠），上面有她亲笔绘制的警卫秘书的女儿隋永清幼年身着朝鲜服装跳舞的画像。

祝賀新年

To Ernest Tang and Family
64 Macdonnell Road
Flat No. 7B
Hongkong
From Soong Ching Ling
Kindness of Lam Kw Tsai 先生

恭賀新年

To wish Mr & Mrs Patrick de Bas
all the best in 1981 and the years to come!
affectionately Soong Ching Ling

宋慶齡

恭賀新年

To Monsieur & Madame Patrick de Bas
Wishing you all the best in 1981!
Soong Ching Ling

宋慶齡

●上排为宋庆龄送给邓广殷一家的贺卡（邓广殷捐赠），为他们送去诚挚的新年祝福；下排是宋庆龄 1980 年连续寄给高醇芳的两张贺年卡，祝福她和新婚丈夫 1981 年及以后每一年都万事如意。

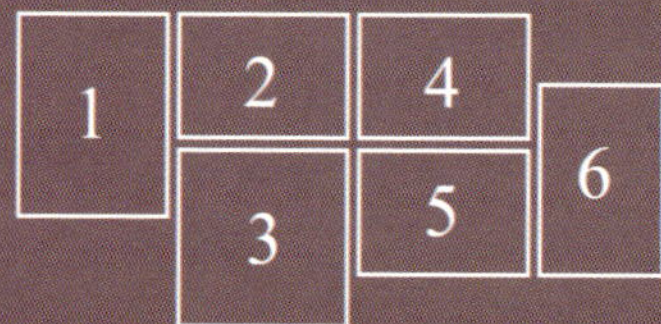

1.1956 年宋庆龄用餐时留影

2.1959 年宋庆龄在上海淮海中路寓所客厅留影

3.1962 年宋庆龄与隋永清合影

4. 宋庆龄在上海淮海中路寓所花园留影

5.1956 年 4 月宋庆龄与李燕娥在上海淮海中路寓所花园留影

6. 宋庆龄在北京寓所鸽棚前留影

1954 年宋庆龄出席第一届全国人民代表大会第一次会议 （薛潮 捐赠）

In 1954, Soong Ching Ling attended the First Session of the First National People's Congress

1956 年宋庆龄应邀参加中国共产党第八次全国代表大会

In 1956, Soong Ching Ling was invited to attend the Eighth National Congress of the Communist Party of China

1959 年宋庆龄出席第二届全国人民代表大会第一次会议

In 1959, Soong Ching Ling attended the First Session of the Second National People's Congress

1959 年宋庆龄出席扩大的最高国务会议
In 1959, Soong Ching Ling attended the expanded Supreme State Conference

1962 年宋庆龄出席最高国务会议
In 1962, Soong Ching Ling attended the Supreme State Conference

人民日报

RENMIN RIBAO

1981年5月
16
星期六
辛酉年四月十三

北京地区天气预报
白天 晴转阴，傍晚有小阵雨
风向 北转南
风力 二、三级
夜间 阴有小阵雨，转晴
风向 南转北
风力 一、二级
温度 最高 25°
最低 14°

国务院作出

社队企业要进行认

本报讯 据新华社报道：国务院5月4日作出关于社队企业贯彻国民经济调整方针的十六条规定。

规定充分肯定了社队企业是农村经济的重要组成部分，符合农村经济综合发展的方向。

规定针对当前社队企业在发展中存在着盲目性，对发挥经济效益和充分利用资源注意不够；在利润使用上生产队和社员直接得到的经济利益偏少；还有不少企业财务管理混乱，不正之风比较严重等问题，指出：社队企业必须贯彻中央关于国民经济实行进一步

中央政治局一致决定
接收宋庆龄同志为中共正式党员

（一九八一年五月十五日）

宋庆龄同志年轻时追随伟大的革命先行者孙中山先生，致力于中国革命事业，从1923年第一次国共两党合作以来，忠贞不渝地坚持孙中山先生革命的新三民主义，在中国长期革命的艰难困苦的斗争中，坚定地和中国共产党站在一起。她一贯是共产党的最亲密战友，是中国各族人民包括台湾同胞和海外侨胞衷心敬爱的领袖之一，是爱国主义、民主主义、国际主义和共产主义的伟大战士，是保卫世界和平事业的久经考验的前驱，是全体中国少年儿童慈爱的祖母。她过去多次要求加入中国共产党，最近病重时又一次提出这个要求。中央政治局一致决定，接收宋庆龄同志为中国共产党正式党员。

（新华社）

中共中央全国人大常委会国务院关于宋庆龄副委员长病情的公告

（第一号）

宋庆龄副委员长患冠心病及慢性淋巴性白血病，经多方治疗，未见好转。曾多次出现发热、呼吸困难、心跳加快等症状。五月十四日晚，突发寒战高热，热度达摄氏四十点二度，伴有严重心力衰竭。目前病情危急，正在积极抢救治疗。

一九八一年五月十五日 （新华社）

宋庆龄同志近照。 新华社记者摄

成都轴承厂实行超额计件计分奖

把奖金与劳动成果和岗位责任制紧密结合起来

四川省委最近向全省工交企业推荐了这个厂的经验

1981年5月15日，中共中央政治局一致决定接收宋庆龄同志为中共正式党员

On May 15, 1981, the Political Bureau of the Central Committee of the Communist Party of China accepted Soong Ching Ling as a full member of the Communist Party of China

人民日報

RENMIN RIBAO

1981年5月
17
星期日
辛酉年四月十四

北京地区天气预报
白天 阴有小阵雨转多云 风向 偏北 风力 一、二级转四级左右
夜间 多云转晴 风向 偏北 风力 一、二级
温度 最高 25° 最低 14°

国营、集体、个体三
乌鲁木齐市商业服

新华社乌鲁木齐5月16日电 新疆乌鲁木齐市采取国营、集体、个体三种经济一齐上的办法，发展商业、服务、修理事业，仅仅一年，就使这个城市的供应面貌改观。

乌鲁木齐市在十年“文化大革命”期间，城市人口增加50%以上，而商业网点却减少了50%。群众买东西、做衣、吃饭、住店都感到困难，就连打酱油醋也得排队。市有关部门原打算由国家新建改建二百多个商业网点。这样做，需要国家投资二千多万元，至少三年才能完成，而且还不能满足群众生活需要。后来，市委决定放开手脚，支持集体、个体经济同国营经济一齐上，

五届全国人大常委会第十八次会议决定
授予宋庆龄中华人民共和国名誉主席荣誉称号

新华社北京5月16日电 第五届全国人民代表大会常务委员会，今天下午在人民大会堂举行第十八次会议，会议通过决定：授予宋庆龄同志中华人民共和国名誉主席的荣誉称号。

会上，邓颖超副委员长转达了中共中央关于授予宋庆龄同志中华人民共和国名誉主席荣誉称号的建议，介绍了宋庆龄同志的革命事迹和入党要求以及党中央接收她为中共正式党员的情况；廖承志副委员长介绍了宋庆龄同志的病况。

会议通过了其他任免事项。

会议由彭真副委员长主持，乌兰夫、韦国清、彭冲、赛福鼎、许德珩、肖劲光、班禅额尔德尼·却吉坚赞副委员长出席了会议。

全国人大常委会关于授予宋庆龄同志中华人民共和国名誉主席荣誉称号的决定

宋庆龄同志是中华人民共和国的缔造者之一，是中国各族人民包括台湾同胞和海外侨胞衷心敬爱的领导人，是举世闻名的爱国主义、民主主义、国际主义、共产主义的伟大战士

新华社北京5月16日电 全国人民代表大会常务委员会关于授予宋庆龄同志中华人民共和国名誉主席荣誉称号的决定

1981年5月16日第五届全国人民代表大会常务委员会第十八次会议通过

宋庆龄同志早年追随伟大的革命家孙中山先生，始终不渝地致力于中国民族解放和人民解放事业，是中华人民共和国的缔造者之一。建国伊始，即被选为中央人民政府副主席；1959年和1965年继续被选为中华人民共和国副主席。七十年来，她一贯在我国人民民主革命和社会主义革命、社会主义建设事业中，坚定地和中国各族人民站在一起，是中国各族人民包括台湾同胞和海外侨胞衷心敬爱的领导人，是举世闻名的爱国主义、民主主义、国际主义、共产主义的伟大战士。她在发展各国人民友好、发扬进步文化、保卫世界和平的事业中，受到中外各方人士的广泛崇敬。宋庆龄同志在我国革命和建设事业中，为国家和人民建立了光辉的业绩。为此，全国人民代表大会常务委员会决定：授予宋庆龄同志中华人民共和国名誉主席的荣誉称号。

中共中央 全国人大常委会 国务院关于宋庆龄副委员长病情的公告

（第二号）

宋庆龄副委员长病情：血白细胞计数由以前的61,700增至158,000，淋巴细胞占91%。15日晚体温达摄氏40.2度，16日白天体温波动于摄氏39度上下。

（新华社）

北京苇坑居委会地区三年无案件

《北京日报》发表文章赞扬苇坑治保积极分子的工作精神

发动群众建立治安保卫网，热情挽救失足青年

本报讯 …真做好治安…这个地区没…北京市治保…心，走路放…

苇坑居…有居民630…辆整天川流…锁，偷盗抢…了治保组织…员包段、积…制订了治保…分子和退休…他们都管。…车357辆。

一天晚…一边留神犄…巢地守在那…二、三十个…明晃晃的匕…械斗即将发…直奔居委会…又返回大院…抓获了流氓…

苇坑居…年。对问题…组成帮教小…内比较有威…广大干部、…

年全管界有六十多名失足青少…名因屡教不改、被送去劳动教…他们中有六名参了军，二名被…

1981 年 5 月 16 日，第五届全国人大常委会第十八次会议接受中共中央政治局的建议，授予宋庆龄中华人民共和国名誉主席荣誉称号

On May 16, 1981, the Eighteenth Session of the Standing Committee of the Fifth National People's Congress accepted the proposal of the Political Bureau of the central committee of the Communist Party of China to confer on Soong Ching Ling the title of Honorary President of the People's Republic of China

1981年5月29日，宋庆龄同志在北京逝世。6月3日下午，追悼大会在人民大会堂隆重举行。邓小平同志在致悼词时指出："宋庆龄同志逝世以前不久，被接收为中国共产党正式党员，实现了她长时期来的夙愿。这是宋庆龄同志的光荣，也是中国共产党的光荣。宋庆龄同志永远活在中国各族人民心中，永远活在中国共产党人心中。"

On May 29, 1981, Soong Ching Ling passed away in Beijing. The memorial meeting was solemnly held in the Great Hall of the People on the afternoon of June 3. In his eulogy, Deng Xiaoping pointed out: "Not long before her death, Soong Ching Ling was accepted as a full member of the Communist Party of China, which fulfilled her long-cherished wish. This is an honor to Soong Ching Ling and to the Communist Party of China. Soong Ching Ling will always live in the hearts of the Chinese people of all nationalities and in the hearts of all members of the Communist Party of China."

宋庆龄同志追悼大会

宋庆龄的坚贞不屈、勇敢忠诚和她的精神的美，

是活的中国最为卓越而辉煌的象征。

SOONG CHING LING'S INCORRUPTIBLE INTEGRITY, COURAGE, LOYALTY, AND BEAUTY OF SPIRIT ARE BURNING SYMBOLS OF THE BEST IN LIVING CHINA.